TAPPING HIDDEN POWER

JOURNEY THROUGH THE MIND AND BODY

TIME® LIFE BOOKS

Other Publications:
WEIGHT WATCHERS® SMART CHOICE RECIPE COLLECTION
TRUE CRIME
THE AMERICAN INDIANS
THE ART OF WOODWORKING
LOST CIVILIZATIONS
ECHOES OF GLORY
THE NEW FACE OF WAR
HOW THINGS WORK
WINGS OF WAR
CREATIVE EVERYDAY COOKING
COLLECTOR'S LIBRARY OF THE UNKNOWN
CLASSICS OF WORLD WAR II
TIME-LIFE LIBRARY OF CURIOUS AND UNUSUAL FACTS
AMERICAN COUNTRY
VOYAGE THROUGH THE UNIVERSE
THE THIRD REICH
THE TIME-LIFE GARDENER'S GUIDE
MYSTERIES OF THE UNKNOWN
TIME FRAME
FIX IT YOURSELF
FITNESS, HEALTH & NUTRITION
SUCCESSFUL PARENTING
HEALTHY HOME COOKING
UNDERSTANDING COMPUTERS
LIBRARY OF NATIONS
THE ENCHANTED WORLD
THE KODAK LIBRARY OF CREATIVE PHOTOGRAPHY
GREAT MEALS IN MINUTES
THE CIVIL WAR
PLANET EARTH
COLLECTOR'S LIBRARY OF THE CIVIL WAR
THE EPIC OF FLIGHT
THE GOOD COOK
WORLD WAR II
HOME REPAIR AND IMPROVEMENT
THE OLD WEST

*For information on and a full description of any of
the Time-Life Books series listed above, please call*
1-800-621-7026 *or write:*
Reader Information
Time-Life Customer Service
P.O. Box C-32068
Richmond, Virginia 23261-2068

TAPPING HIDDEN POWER

JOURNEY THROUGH THE MIND AND BODY

BY THE EDITORS OF TIME-LIFE BOOKS
ALEXANDRIA, VIRGINIA

CONSULTANTS:

HUDA AKIL has explored many aspects of opioids, including their pharmacology and their molecular structure. She is director of the Neuroscience Graduate Program at the University of Michigan.

MARGARET CAUDILL, an internist and pain consultant, is director of the Behavioral Medicine Pain Clinic at the Hitchcock Clinic, Nashua, N.H., and codirector of the Arnold Pain Center in the division of behavioral medicine at the New England Deaconess Hospital, Boston.

RONALD DUBNER is chief of the Neurobiology and Anesthesiology branch of the National Institute of Dental Research in Bethesda, Maryland. His research involving many aspects of the control of pain includes new pharmacological strategies.

THOMAS MASTROIANNI is a pianist and chairman of the music department at Catholic University, Washington, D.C., where he teaches courses related to arts and medicine. He founded an arts-medicine clinic in the D.C. area.

JAMES E. MITCHELL is currently chief of the Psychology Service at the United States Air Force Survival School in Spokane, Washington.

SHANE MURPHY, a sport psychologist, is associate director of the United States Olympic Committee's Division of Sport Science and Technology.

CLARK T. SAWIN is chief of the endocrine-diabetes section of the Veterans Affairs Medical Center in Boston. He has an academic appointment at Tufts University School of Medicine.

JOURNEY THROUGH THE MIND AND BODY

Time-Life Books is a division of
TIME LIFE INC.

PRESIDENT AND CEO: John M. Fahey Jr.

EDITOR-IN-CHIEF: John L. Papanek

TIME-LIFE BOOKS

MANAGING EDITOR: Roberta Conlan
Executive Art Director: Ellen Robling
Director of Photography and Research:
    John Conrad Weiser
Senior Editors: Russell B. Adams Jr., Dale M.
    Brown, Janet Cave, Lee Hassig, Robert
    Somerville, Henry Woodhead
Director of Technology: Eileen Bradley
Director of Editorial Operations:
    Prudence G. Harris

PRESIDENT: John D. Hall

Vice President, Director of Marketing:
    Nancy K. Jones
Vice President, New Product Development:
    Neil Kagan
Director of Production Services: Robert N. Carr
Production Manager: Marlene Zack
Supervisor of Quality Control: James King

Editorial Operations
Production: Celia Beattie
Library: Louise D. Forstall
Computer Composition: Deborah G. Tait
    (Manager), Monika D. Thayer, Janet
    Barnes Syring, Lillian Daniels

SERIES EDITOR: Robert Somerville
Administrative Editor: Judith W. Shanks

Editorial Staff for *Tapping Hidden Power*
Art Directors: Rebecca Mowrey, Barbara
    Sheppard, Fatima Taylor
Picture Editor: Kristin Baker Hanneman
Text Editors: Jim Watson (principal), Carl
    Posey
Associate Editors/Research and Writing: Ruth
    Goldberg, Mark Rogers
Assistant Editor/Research: M. Kevan Miller
Copyeditor: Donna D. Carey
Editorial Assistant: Kris Dittman
Picture Coordinator: Paige Henke

Special Contributors:
George Constable, Peter Copeland, Juli
Duncan, Laura Foreman, Gina Maranto,
Peter Pocock, Bruce Selcraig, Mark Wash-
burn, Elizabeth Winters (text); Vilasini
Balakrishnan, Nancy Blodgett, Susan Blair,
Gretchen Case, Anna Gedrich, Stephanie
Henke (research); Barbara L. Klein (index);
John Drummond (design).

Correspondents:
Christine Hinze (London); Juan Sosa, John
H. Strait (Moscow); Christina Lieberman
(New York); Maria Vincenza Aloisi (Paris);
Michael Donath (Prague); Ann Natanson
(Rome). Valuable assistance was also pro-
vided by Trini Bandrés (Madrid); Elizabeth
Brown, Dan Donnelly (New York); Ann Wise
(Rome); and Bogdan Turek (Warsaw).

Library of Congress
Cataloging-in-Publication Data
Tapping Hidden Power/by the editors of
Time-Life Books.
    p. cm.— (Journey through the mind and
body)
    Includes bibliographical references and
index.
    ISBN 0-7835-1052-7 (trade)
    ISBN 0-7835-1053-5 (library)
1. Mind and Body. 2. Adaptability (Psychology). 3. New thought. 4. Stress management.   I. Time-Life Books.   II. Series.
BF161.T19 1994
158'.1— dc20   94-430

First printing. Printed in U.S.A.
Published simultaneously in Canada.
School and library distribution by
Time-Life Education, P.O. Box 85026,
Richmond, Virginia 23285-5026.

TIME-LIFE is a trademark of Time Warner
Inc. U.S.A.

This volume is one of a series that
explores the fascinating inner universe
of the human mind and body.

CONTENTS

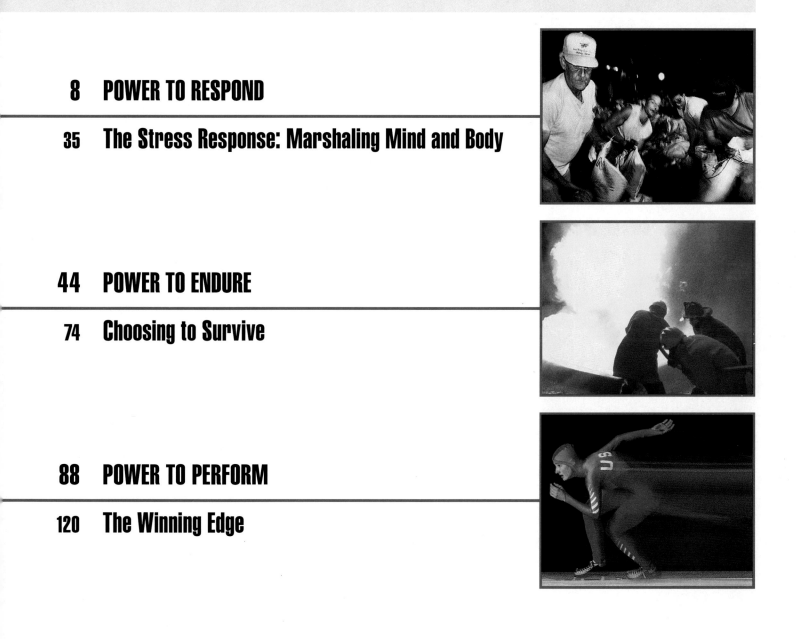

1

Power to Respond

What began as a routine recreational parachute jump turned in a moment into a nightmare. On Easter weekend in 1987, Gregory Robertson, a veteran skydiving instructor with more than 1,700 dives to his credit, had joined six other jumpers in an attempt to form a hand-to-hand ring in the skies above Coolidge, Arizona. Although the move was tricky, it was not especially dangerous for experienced free-fallers. The group managed to complete the airborne circle and were beginning to split apart when disaster struck. Debbie Williams, a 31-year-old elementary schoolteacher who had made 50 jumps, smashed headfirst into the backpack of another diver at a relative speed of 50 miles per hour. The collision left Williams unconscious and helplessly spinning earthward at 160 miles per hour.

From his position above the rest of the group, Robertson watched the accident and knew that unless someone acted quickly, Williams would die. "I just couldn't let that happen," he said later. At a moment when others might have panicked, Robertson performed with cool, deliberate precision. He pulled in his arms and legs, streamlining himself to accelerate his descent rate to more than 200 miles per hour. As he overtook the helpless Williams, Robertson spread his

arms and legs to increase wind resistance and slow down. With one hand, he grabbed Williams's harness; with the other, he pulled the rip cord to release her parachute. Then, at an altitude of 2,000 feet—seven seconds from impact—Robertson opened his own chute. Still unconscious, Debbie Williams hit the ground roughly, suffering a fractured skull, nine broken ribs, and a perforated kidney. But six months after the harrowing incident, she returned to the sport she loved, accompanied by the man who had saved her life.

Gregory Robertson's quick thinking and physical dexterity had averted a tragedy. Yet Robertson was no superman. Like most heroes, he was an ordinary person who, at a moment of supreme challenge, had summoned the mental and physical resources the situation demanded. Admittedly, his experience as an instructor had endowed him with abilities and a level of confidence that no doubt helped him carry out the heroic deed. Even so, his almost unconscious decision to act, combined with his acute presence of mind in the face of danger, demonstrates the remarkable power of the human response system. In times of crisis, some people find themselves able to exceed their normal limitations, surmounting fear and self-doubt to perform seemingly impossible feats of strength, endurance, or mental prowess. Not everyone has the makings of a hero, of course. But all human beings have within them the ability to draw energy from these inner reserves and achieve higher levels of performance.

No one knows exactly what turns some people into heroes and others into bystanders—why some individuals bravely hurl themselves at danger while others freeze with apprehension. But in recent years, scientists at the forefront of research into the workings of the mind and body have shed new light on the complex series of reactions that fuel human response. As they have discovered, sources of power hidden within us all work at both conscious and unconscious levels to meet a wide range of challenges, from deadly peril to the vicissitudes of everyday life.

Most of the time, people are unaware of the routine functions of their own body. When a particular demand arises—say, for a burst of energy, enhanced alertness, or simply a period of healing rest—myriad physiological systems within the body go to work automatically, without conscious intervention. And yet, some individuals seem able to activate these systems more or less at will.

The ability to engage the body's internal machinery essentially on demand is rare, but virtually everyone can learn techniques that enhance physical and mental performance. Many athletes, for example, have increased their speed, strength, and endurance merely by harnessing their powers of concentration. In fact, performers of every stripe—from musicians, dancers, and actors to salespeople, chefs, and teachers—have found similar ways to surpass their normal standards.

Some have gained access to profound wellsprings of energy and confidence through such time-honored practices as meditation; others have taken advantage of newer methods that make use of some of the most sophisticated tools of modern science. But in any case, the benefits of tapping that hidden power are clear, helping us to improve our lives—and perhaps even to save them.

Trained professionals such as Gregory Robertson seem to come equipped for heroic pursuits, but bursts of extraordinary ability sometimes make heroes out of those who are least prepared. Helen Miller, a young mother with three preschool children, lived by the bank of a swiftly flowing stream in Oregon. She had never learned to swim and, in fact, had a great fear of water. One day in 1954,

Gregory Robertson *(left, in black)* and two other skydiving instructors link up during a free-fall exercise over Coolidge, Arizona, near the site of Robertson's daring last-second rescue of fellow skydiver Debbie Williams one year later. A few weeks after the 1987 incident, Williams looks on from her hospital bed in Texas by way of a television monitor *(below)* as Robertson, in New York City, shows off a medal he received for his heroics.

about a month after an accident had left her right hand bandaged and nearly useless, Miller's five-year-old daughter, Benicia, told her that three-year-old Marijane had gone down to the creek to "catch a duckie." Terrified, Miller dashed to the creek to discover that the bank was empty. "From that moment on," as she later described the episode, "my mind is divorced from my body. It has no weight, no feeling, no sense of time or distance . . . only blind, unreasoning, suffocating fear."

Spotting her daughter in the stream, Miller plunged into the frigid, swirling waters. Her feet could not touch bottom. Desperately, she grabbed with her good hand at roots dangling from the bank while straining to reach Marijane with her injured hand. All thoughts of how handicapped she had been left her. "Now there is no pain, no weakness," she said, reliving the moment. "My hand touches Janie, lifts her just above the surface." The stream bank was two feet above her head, but Miller effortlessly tossed the little girl up near its edge, only to see her slide back down into the water. Again, the woman threw her child up over the embankment, this time successfully, then managed to pull herself out of the current to safety. As she lay there bleeding, frozen, and in shock, all that mattered to her was that she had saved her daughter's life.

Although her ability to respond was well-nigh inexplicable, Helen Miller's motivation was not: Her little girl was in peril, and probably nothing would have stopped her. Perhaps more extraordinary are the heroic acts that spring from less-instinctive urges, as in the case of Lucille Babcock. A white-haired, bespectacled poet in her sixties who walked with the aid of a cane, Babcock was doing chores in her second-floor apartment in Little Rock, Arkansas, one morning in 1987 when she heard a scream outside. From her window, she saw a man attacking her 22-year-old neighbor, dragging her across the yard. Babcock

grabbed her cane and hurried downstairs to find the man pinning his victim to the ground and clawing at her clothes. "I'm a policeman!" the older woman shouted, in an effort to scare off the attacker. "Get off her!"

The man did not respond, so Babcock began whaling away at him with her cane. He got up and ran to his car, but Babcock followed, her cane still swinging. When the man opened his car door, Babcock slammed it shut, smashing his knees. The would-be rapist then tried to flee on foot but was soon apprehended by three other people nearby. Later, Little Rock police officials praised Lucille Babcock for her heroism. "I am not a hero," came her reply. "I just can't stand to see people being hurt."

Gary Hutzell, a 41-year-old home-

In a scene broadcast live on national television, Lenny Skutnik pulls Priscilla Tirado to safety after the Air Florida jetliner on which she had been a passenger crashed and sank into the Potomac River near Washington, D.C., on January 13, 1982. Of the hundreds of people at the scene, only Skutnik and one other man dared the icy water in rescue efforts.

improvement contractor in Vienna, Virginia, apparently shares that aversion. Late one night in the early 1970s, while he was driving along a winding country road, Hutzell came upon the aftermath of a recent collision between a compact car and a motorcycle. He stopped to offer assistance and discovered that the impact of the crash had hurled the motorcyclist safely, if painfully, into a ditch. Then Hutzell noticed something else: a shape lying under the car.

Looking closely, he could see it was a young woman—the motorcycle's passenger, as it turned out—wedged facedown between the engine and the pavement. Without pausing to think, Hutzell ran to the rear of the car, grabbed the bumper, and raised the back end off the ground. He staggered several feet forward with the 2,500-pound automobile, stepping over the woman as he walked, then set it down out of harm's way. He waited with the victim at the accident site until an ambulance, summoned by the driver of the car, arrived.

Although she was severely injured, the woman survived. She had been rescued by a man who was five feet six inches tall and, at the time of the accident, weighed only about 150

pounds. His extraordinary strength during the emergency seemed to have exploded out of nowhere and was carried on a wave of supreme self-confidence. He did not stop to wonder if he was strong enough to pick up a car. As he recalled the incident, "There was no question in my mind that it was going to happen."

Such heroic performances owe in part to the effects of epinephrine, better known as adrenaline, a hormone that is released into the bloodstream by the adrenal glands just above the kidneys. Many people are familiar with the so-called adrenaline rush that occurs in moments of excitement or fear, as the heart suddenly begins to race, pumping blood more quickly to enable the body to meet the needs of the moment.

But epinephrine does not act alone, nor does it burst into action only in moments of crisis. It is one of many elements in a complex response system that serves as the body's standard arsenal for dealing with stress. Indeed, evolution has shaped the human body to cope with a wide range of stressful influences, most of them so mundane that they escape conscious detection. Every day, the autonomic nervous system and hormone-distributing neuroendocrine system (*pages* 35-43) orchestrate thousands of biochemical reactions that the body needs to meet even the most routine

of life's challenges. Within the past century, new insights have emerged about the functions of these complex systems—insights rooted in a quest that began long ago for the elusive connection between the physical body and the intangible mind.

Since ancient times, healers and practitioners of the medical arts have struggled to understand the labyrinthine workings of the human body. To many, the answer to this enormously complex puzzle seemed to lie in elucidating the sources of disease and the nature of health. The Greek scholar Hippocrates, widely acknowledged as the father of medicine, told his students in the fifth century BC that disease was not only suffering (*pathos*), but also toil (*ponos*), as the body fought to return to a normal condition. But what was the exact nature of this toil? Hippocrates himself posed the question, but it would be centuries before an answer would begin to take shape.

In 1870 the great French physiologist Claude Bernard took one of the first big steps toward that answer when he announced his concept of the *milieu intérieur*—the "internal environment" that exists within all living organisms.

Pioneer researchers Walter Cannon *(right)* and Hans Selye *(below)* mapped out the course of modern investigations into the body's response to stress. In 1926 Cannon proposed that the body strives to maintain a state of internal stability, or homeostasis. A decade later, Selye published his breakthrough theory that, when homeostasis has been disrupted, the body seeks to restore its internal balance through a series of reactions that he termed the general adaptation syndrome.

"It is the fixity of the internal environment that is the condition of free and independent life," he wrote in 1857. All organisms, "however varied they may be," Bernard argued, work to maintain a constant internal environment that is always in balance with itself and with the surrounding world. In human beings, for example, the internal temperature of a healthy individual always hovers within a certain range near 98 degrees Fahrenheit, whether that person lives in the Tropics or the Arctic. (Recent research indicates that 98.2 is closer to the average than 98.6.) Likewise, the composition of the blood changes very little, and only for short periods of time. The French scientist contended that organisms, particularly those that are more complex, possess internal control systems that constantly adjust bodily functions in order to maintain a stable milieu interieur.

The notion of a well-regulated internal environment became one of the foundation stones of modern medicine, but it took the work of another scientist, American physiologist Walter B. Cannon, to develop Bernard's concept and bring its full significance to light. Born in Prairie du Chien, Wisconsin, in 1871, Cannon was a man with a special ability to combine research skills with an imaginative application of scholarship. In 1896, his first year as a medical student at Har-

vard, he used the brand-new technique of x-rays to study the process of swallowing and digestion in geese and cats. He discovered there was also much to learn from examining subjects much closer at hand. "In 1905," he wrote in his memoirs years later, "while observing in myself the rhythmic sounds produced by the activities of the alimentary tract, I had occasion to note that the sensation of hunger was not constant but recurrent, and that the moment of its disappearance was often associated with a rather loud gurgling sound as heard through the stethoscope." One of Cannon's most famous books, *The Wisdom of the Body*, reflected this and other insights about what was going on inside the body and how it went about governing its own environment.

Elaborating on Bernard's original concept, Cannon came up with a term for the process of internal regulation: homeostasis, from the Greek words *homoios*, meaning same or similar, and *stasis*, for position or standing. Homeostasis therefore might be translated as "staying power," or the body's relentless effort to maintain its integrity. "The living being is stable," Cannon once wrote. "It must be so in order not to be destroyed, dissolved or dis-

integrated by the colossal forces, often adverse, which surround it."

Homeostatic regulation goes on all the time, as when the body perspires in order to cool itself down after exertion heats it up. But perhaps more revealing of the mechanisms involved are cases in which the balance is deliberately upset. During World War I, Cannon began to examine just such a set of circumstances in a study of soldiers suffering from traumatic shock. His findings, combined with results from subsequent experiments on animals, led him to conclude that in life-threatening situations the body organizes its resources and sets in motion a host of complex reactions designed to help the body either confront the threat or escape from it. Cannon dubbed this the fight-or-flight response, and he realized that it leads to drastic alterations in homeostasis.

The fight-or-flight response includes an increase in metabolism, or the rate at which the body consumes oxygen, as well as changes in breathing, blood pressure, heart rate, and the volume of blood that is pumped by the heart and delivered to the skeletal muscles. The body rallies to meet the emergency as if summoned by a bugle call. But Cannon was unable to answer the most important question: Who blows the bugle?

As it happened, the solution to this puzzle fell to physiologist Walter R.

Hess, a Swiss Nobel laureate who during the 1920s and 1930s extended Cannon's work through experiments on the brains of cats. Hess discovered that when he stimulated the hypothalamus, an olive-size structure at the base of the brain, the body immediately went into its fight-or-flight response. Thus was revealed the brain's elusive bugler. When a cat sees a dog—or when Lucille Babcock sees a mugger—this tiny element sounds the alarm and mobilizes the body's resources to meet the emergency.

However, it would soon become clear that the body's response to such situations is not limited to an all-out fight-or-flight reaction, nor does it always work to the good. In 1925 Hans Selye, a 19-year-old medical student at the German University of Prague, prepared for the moment of truth that must be faced by any prospective doctor. Having completed his coursework in subjects such as anatomy and biochemistry, he was about to meet his first actual patients. When his professor presented the budding physicians with patients in the earliest stages of various infectious diseases, Selye was struck by a curious fact: Although the patients as yet manifested few specific symptoms of disease,

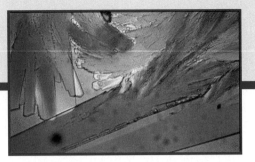

A Wonder Drug's Hideous Strength

In the 1950s, researchers hailed the development of a surgical anesthetic called phencyclidine, shown in crystalline form above, which was intended to be used to suppress the perception of pain in cases where doctors wanted to avoid full anesthesia. Over time, however, scientists noticed disturbing side effects in test subjects, such as agitation, auditory hallucinations, fearful delusions, psychosis, and catatonia.

Tests on humans were halted in the early 1960s, but within two years phencyclidine had hit the streets, where it has since acquired a variety of nicknames, including PCP, angel dust, and DOA (dead on arrival). Many users seek the out-of-body sensation that they claim is brought on by PCP, although in reality the effects of the drug can differ from one occasion to another and are impossible to predict.

In some people, PCP creates a sense of invincibility and superhuman strength, perhaps because it masks pain that otherwise might deter certain actions. The effects are more than imaginary: PCP users have been known to exert enough pressure with their arms to break out of steel handcuffs, snapping their wrists in the process. Such cases have prompted many officials to adopt a "one person per limb" policy (right) for restraining those under the drug's influence.

Some scientists think PCP may boost strength by stimulating the release of the hormone norepinephrine, thereby setting off a chain of reactions similar to those that occur during the body's natural fight-or-flight response.

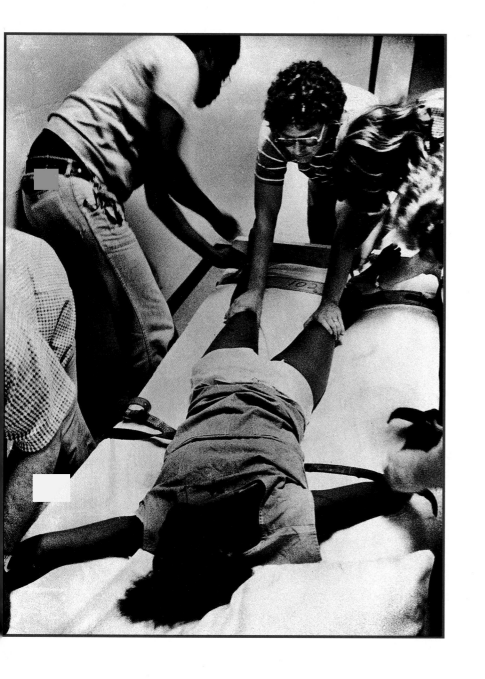

they all appeared exhausted, dispirited, and drawn. However, to the young observer's surprise, the professor regarded these symptoms as unimportant. "Since these were my first patients," Selye later wrote, "I was still capable of looking at them without being biased by current medical thought. Had I known more, I would never have asked myself questions."

In his youthful ignorance, Selye found himself wondering why the professor paid no attention to the patients' nonspecific symptoms—the manifestations of literal "dis-ease" that typically accompany illness. "I could not understand why, ever since the dawn of medical history, physicians should have attempted to concentrate all their efforts upon the recognition of individual diseases and the discovery of specific remedies for them, without giving any attention to the much more obvious syndrome of 'just being sick.'" When he raised the point with his professor, the older man simply laughed and advised him to leave such theorizing to those with experience. Selye put the idea aside and devoted himself to the very specific matter of passing his exams.

A decade later, as an assistant in the biochemistry department at McGill

University in Montreal, Selye was attempting to isolate a new hormone by injecting rats with certain extracts of the ovarian glands and placenta. During the course of his experiments, he found that the animals experienced three distinct reactions to the extracts: The adrenal cortex, or the outer portion of the adrenal glands, grew larger; parts of the immune system, including the spleen and lymph nodes, atrophied; and stomach ulcers appeared. Exultantly, Selye believed he was indeed on the verge of identifying a new hormone produced by the ovaries, a single chemical responsible for the syndrome, or set of related effects, he had observed. But further experiments showed that extracts from a host of other organs, including some that were not thought to manufacture ovarian hormones, yielded exactly the same results. Apparently the new hormone did not exist, after all.

But the syndrome itself certainly did. The scientist's thoughts returned to the notion of a "syndrome of just being sick." He wondered if there could be an integrated response to any assault, such as disease or even the intrusions of a medical experimenter. "If this were so," Selye wrote, "the general medical implications of the syndrome would be enormous!" It would mean that all previous studies of the effects of diseases and drugs had been flawed because they blindly lumped together the specific effects of a particular disease or drug with the general, nonspecific effects of this presumed response syndrome.

Selye began to realize that it was impossible to evaluate the overall effect of a specific influence on the body without taking into account the nonspecific response as well. Conventional scientific wisdom of the day held that each agent triggered a separate physical reaction, so many of Selye's colleagues brushed aside his idea of a sweeping, generic, one-size-fits-all response. But as Selye continued his research, his confidence was buoyed by consistent results. As he wrote, "I could find no noxious agent that did not produce the syndrome." The importance of this revelation was clear to Selye, who wrote up a brief, 74-line article that appeared in the July 1936 issue of the prestigious British journal *Nature*. Much more was to follow. Since then, more than 100,000 articles and books have been written about what Selye called the general adaptation syndrome. Selye himself penned some 1,600 articles and 30 books on the subject.

In his writings and discussions, Selye began to refer to the general adaptation syndrome in terms of stress.

The term *stress* had long been used in engineering and physics to indicate the effects of a force acting against resistance, such as the stress on a rubber band as it is stretched. Now Hans Selye applied the expression to biological processes as well, and before long it was extended to cover psychological factors.

Selye defined stress as "the nonspecific response of the body to any demand made upon it." However, this definition turned out to be so broad that it could include virtually anything, from the annoying clang of an alarm clock to terminal cancer. So Selye came up with the term *distress* to describe harmful stress, *eustress* (from the Greek prefix *eu*, meaning "good") to describe productive or beneficial stress, and *stressor* to describe the agent that actually produced the stress response. If, by this measure, a worker's boss yells at him to get a job done sooner, and the worker responds by getting an upset stomach as he works faster, the boss is the stressor, the reaction that speeds the work is eustress, and the unpleasant digestive response is distress.

To many people, the word *stress* has, by definition, a distinctly negative flavor. But as Selye pointed out, stress is a natural and essential part of the human experience. "Stress," as he put it, "is not even necessarily bad for you; it is also the spice of life, for any emotion, any activity causes stress." Just as the whine of a dentist's drill can be stressful, according to Selye, so can a passionate kiss; both tend to raise blood pressure, quicken respiration, and boost the heart rate. "And yet who in the world would forgo such a pleasurable pastime simply because of the stress involved?" Thus the goal, in Selye's view, should not be to avoid experiencing stress, but to adopt a new attitude toward events, converting negative perceptions into positive ones, distress into eustress.

As researchers soon learned, the process of the general adaptation syndrome is controlled by the autonomic nervous system, a complex network made up of two complementary subsystems. In simple terms, the sympathetic system serves as the instigator, delivering signals that stir the body into action. The parasympathetic system counteracts the response and helps restore homeostasis. These systems work together in three distinct phases that Selye himself identified: an immediate alarm reaction, which was Cannon's fight-or-flight response; a similar but more enduring reaction called resistance; and finally exhaustion, the stage when the effects of prolonged stress manifest themselves.

If the alarm stage of the general adaptation syndrome represents the body's rallying cry and first alert to danger, the resistance phase can be thought of as the secondary response to attack, the conversion from a peacetime to a wartime economy. Just as a nation under siege hunkers down for battle, the body activates its forces during resistance and gears up for a prolonged period of stress. Eventually, though, like a country that has been at war too long, the weary body begins to break down under the unyielding stress.

Exhaustion, the final phase of the general adaptation syndrome, is the result of prolonged resistance reactions and a consequent inability of the body to restore homeostasis. According to Selye's theory, changes such as elevated blood pressure that provide short-term benefits may over time produce detrimental effects, such as hypertension. Some studies have suggested how this may work at the molecular level. During the resistance phase, for example, certain hormones come into play that help to supply energy by converting amino acids—the building blocks of protein —into glucose. But if the resistance phase continues, these hormones become depleted, blood sugar levels drop, and body cells are deprived of vital nutrients. Other results of prolonged stress include weakening of

such organs as the heart through overwork, and the formation of stomach ulcers, as Selye had observed in his experiments with laboratory rats.

Some scientists have argued with Selye's explanation of the specific mechanisms of exhaustion, but there is little disagreement about the existence of such a stage. A further question remains, however. Why should such an exquisitely orchestrated protective strategy include such negative effects? The answer may lie in the changing nature of the threats we face.

Like so much else about us, the syndrome that Hans Selye envisioned presumably developed through a long process of evolution that wrought gradual changes in organisms as they adapted to meet the challenge of surviving in a dangerous world. Whereas organic evolution is slow, however, the evolution of human society has been breathtakingly rapid. The fight-or-flight response that enabled our ancestors to prevail over wild predators and other physical threats has not itself adapted to a world where common stressors, such as traffic jams and high-pressure jobs, typically cannot be allayed by either fighting or fleeing. Today, stressful situations are not limited to immediate hazards to life and limb, but also include such enduring concerns as job security, healthcare, and even social acceptance. As the causes of stress have changed, then, so must the strategies people use to cope with it.

At the root of our sometimes misguided responses is the fact that the sources of stress often lie within us rather than around us, playing off our attitudes and expectations and our overall state of mind. In some cases, a threat great enough to spark a stressful response exists purely in the imagination. At other times, a close brush with real peril or a misperception of danger sets off and, perhaps, sustains physical reactions far beyond any useful purpose.

Instances of what might be called a useless stress response can be relatively common in modern life. A driver involved in a near miss on the highway may find her heart racing uncontrollably, sweat pouring from her brow, her knuckles turning white as she clutches the wheel. She may be so affected by the incident that she feels momentarily paralyzed and unable to operate her car properly. As the hormones of the alarm reaction continue to course through her, her body and mind remain gripped in the thrall of the fight-or-flight response, which has done nothing to help her deal with the situation but has instead

The Stresses of Modern-Day Life

actually interfered with abilities she needs in the aftermath.

Such an experience illustrates the enormous role the mind plays in the body's stress response. In this case, the driver was reacting to a potential threat that quickly passed. But the same kind of response can be elicited

when the danger is more perceived than real. A backfiring car or any sort of loud bang, for example, could trigger the stress response in a soldier or a police officer, who might interpret the noise as a gunshot: There was, in reality, no danger at all. Or the threat might be completely divorced from the physical realm, and could be either real or imagined, such as a downturn in the stock market or a groundless rumor of layoffs at work: In either

case, a physical reaction provides absolutely no antidote at all. Even when no actual threat exists, if the mind believes one does, the body will respond accordingly.

The mind's power to engender stress in the body was vividly demonstrated to Atlanta psychologist John J. Parrino while he was treating a patient named Richard in the 1970s. Richard was a high-level executive for a small company and had a wife and two children. His marriage was troubled, and his business involved un-

ceasing pressure. He began to suffer from extreme anxiety and states of panic, his blood pressure fluctuated dramatically, he experienced spells of dizziness, and he was unable to concentrate. His doctor hospitalized him for what was diagnosed as a severe stress reaction, and his case came to Parrino's attention.

In the course of one examination, Parrino attached a device to one of Richard's fingers that measured blood flow, then asked the patient to imagine a quiet, pleasant scene. The finger pulse readings appeared normal. Then the psychologist asked Richard to imagine a phone call from his wife. Immediately, blood flow to the man's

skin declined—precisely as it would during the alarm reaction stage of the general adaptation syndrome. The mere suggestion of other stressful situations produced a similar response. Richard's body was reacting to imaginary stimuli in exactly the same way that his ancestors might have reacted to the very real attack of a wild beast.

Evidence from cases such as Richard's has led many researchers, Parrino among them, to conclude that Selye's general adaptation syndrome is only one part of a larger, much more

Pollutants dumped into the air by factories and power plants *(left)* have been implicated in a wide range of health problems, including interfering with the homeostatic mechanisms that help control the stress response.

Inured to horror, a woman in Moscow makes a telephone call near the body of a person killed during the October 1993 rebellion in the Russian capital. Like many who live in war-torn environments, she has apparently learned to cope with extraordinary stress as she goes about daily routines.

complex reaction. Parrino, in fact, has proposed a more comprehensive process called the human response system, which he describes as "the apparatus that handles the various life events that we encounter as humans." In other words, we are equipped for reacting to a broad range of experiences, not just physical threats, and our reactions are not just physiological. The three primary components of the human response system, as Parrino sees it, are thought, physiological responses (essentially the general adaptation syndrome), and behavior.

Since thoughts cannot be observed, and physiological responses involve complicated measurements, Parrino

has focused primarily on the third component, behavior, which is readily observable. He draws a sharp distinction between two types of behavior, adaptive and maladaptive. In adaptive behavior, individuals find productive ways to cope with the stress reaction and use it to their advantage. In maladaptive behavior, people become trapped in a kind of vicious circle of reactions and counterreactions, engaging in activities that tend to reinforce or perpetuate the original stress response. As Parrino explains

in his book *From Panic to Power*, a significant barometer for measuring one's adaptability is emotion. "Pleasant feelings," he writes, "can provide a signal to the system that human responses and coping strategies are adaptive. Unpleasant emotions, in turn, are warning signals of a maladaptive strategy of living."

Parrino argues that the mind, like the body, seeks to maintain a type of equilibrium, or homeostasis, and that all three aspects of the human response system—thoughts and behavior in addition to physiological response—take part. But any analysis of the various forms of this inherent

balancing act must begin with an understanding of the key role played in homeostasis by the autonomic nervous system and its two components, the sympathetic and parasympathetic systems. Although these two subsystems work together to regulate the internal environment, the parasympathetic takes the lead in restoring equilibrium when the body has been called into action.

The functions of this inhibiting branch of the autonomic nervous system are mediated through the vagus nerve, a network of fibers connected to the brainstem that serves as the main highway for instructions from the brain to the heart and to other parts of the parasympathetic nervous system. By the early 19th century, scientists knew that electrical stimulation of the vagus nerve slowed the beating of a frog's heart. In 1921, however, German pharmacologist Otto Loewi demonstrated that the actual mechanism that slowed the heart was not electrical in nature, but chemical.

In his laboratory, Loewi electrically stimulated one frog's vagus nerve and observed the expected slowdown in the beating of its heart. Then he extracted some of the fluid surrounding that creature's heart and used it to bathe the heart of another frog. Frog Number Two's heart immediately slowed down, proving that the message had to have been transmitted chemically. The precise chemical turned out to be a substance called acetylcholine. Since Loewi's day, scientists have established that heart rate, or the number of times the organ beats per minute, is determined through the continuous interplay of both branches of the autonomic nervous system. The sympathetic branch speeds up the heart by stimulating the muscle tissue with bursts of epinephrine. The parasympathetic system then uses secretions of inhibiting acetylcholine to bring the rate back down to its normal level.

This exquisite partnership plays an important role in regulating a number of other functions throughout the body. Besides slowing the heart rate, the parasympathetic system also works to reverse many other effects of the alarm reaction. It relaxes the muscles of the digestive system; constricts the respiratory passages, the iris, and the bladder; and in general prepares the body for a period of rest and recuperation following the fight-or-flight response.

The sympathetic and parasympathetic nervous systems are more than just complementary opposites; both are active, to some degree, at all times. In fact, during the stress reaction, either may rise to play the dominant role. This explains why some people (and animals), when confronted with peril, simply faint rather than fight or flee. This response, known as syncope, results from a lack of blood reaching the brain (due primarily to actions of the central nervous system but with an exacerbating contribution by the parasympathetic system involving a sudden lowering of blood pressure). Parasympathetic constriction of bronchial passages may induce an

asthma attack at times of great stress.

Stress occurring over long periods of time may create in some individuals lethargy, depression, or a tendency to become overweight. Some researchers speculate that such conditions may come about because the parasympathetic system has repressed normal stimulation of the thyroid gland, inhibiting the release of metabolism-stoking hormones. Even in the short run, extreme stress can have dire consequences. It is literally possible, for example, to scare someone to death, but other kinds of stress can produce the same result. Highly emotional situations—say, the loss of a loved one, the anniversary of such a loss, or even a moment of great triumph—can in rare instances trigger such a strong response that a person's heart abruptly stops beating. At such moments, the normal reciprocity of the sympathetic and parasympathetic systems has apparently broken down, overwhelming the body with hyperstimulation of one system or the other or with the combined actions of both.

It is difficult to predict precisely how a given individual's body will react in a crisis, and even more difficult—if not impossible—to mitigate harmful responses that kick in some-

times within fractions of a second. By contrast, although we may not be physically adapted to handling more enduring threats, our responses to chronic stress can be controlled in ways that the sudden alarm reaction cannot. Over the years, scientists have identified many of the factors that are involved in long-term stress and, in the process, devised strategies for minimizing its deleterious effects.

There is, perhaps, no more stressful human activity than warfare. Soldiers who have been at the front too long may go berserk or simply collapse, falling victim to various forms of mental or physical paralysis. The blank look of despair in the eyes of war-weary combat veterans—sometimes known as the thousand-yard stare—is a familiar external manifestation of the psychological toll of battle (page 26). During the Civil War, doctors referred to the affliction as "nostalgia" and considered it a form of insanity. The seemingly endless trench warfare of World War I produced untold numbers of cases of what was then called shell shock. Physicians theorized that the concussion of artillery had actually caused some kind of brain damage. By World War II, the shell shock theory had been abandoned, and the condition was diagnosed as combat psychoneurosis, categorized as a type of mental illness. Further study suggest-

The dazed "thousand-yard stare" of a World War II soldier reveals the harsh toll that warfare can take on the mind as well as the body. Like many of his fellow servicemen, this man suffered from what was known at the time as combat psychoneurosis, a condition now diagnosed as posttraumatic stress syndrome.

ed yet another relatively uninformative label, that of combat fatigue. The condition is now generally known as posttraumatic stress syndrome and has been shown to affect not only victims of warfare and its participants but also anyone who has been subjected to an extremely stressful situation such as a fire or automobile accident or the like. For soldiers in particular, though, prolonged, unrelieved stress was as often the culprit as sudden trauma.

By the time of the Vietnam War, the American military had made some progress in coping with such stress reactions. Psychologists who studied the problem found that the key to averting combat fatigue lay in providing opportunities for soldiers to recover from the effects of prolonged stress. Circumstances provided as much help as any deliberate strategy. Because of the way this particular war was fought, units often spent a day or two in the field, then were plucked out of the jungle by helicopter and carried to a safe area. There, the GIs could relax, drink beer, eat steak, take hot showers, and watch movies. And unlike the situation in previous wars, when a soldier might remain in action for the duration of the conflict, the tour of duty in Vietnam was limited to 13 months; weary troops therefore could count the days remaining until their stress would be relieved. All of these factors dramatically reduced the incidence of combat fatigue among American forces in Vietnam. During the war's peak years, fewer than 100 cases were reported each year.

The lessons of warfare have been applied with a fair measure of success to civilian life. When the record-breaking floods of 1993 inundated vast areas of the American Midwest, disaster-relief teams included psychiatric nurses, psychologists, and specially trained counselors. For those who spent weeks on end sandbagging levees in an often vain effort to save their homes and towns, the flood amounted to the equivalent of war, and the stress was no less severe. People such as these, forced to endure long stints of unremitting hardship, suffer prolonged "depression, sadness, and feelings of hopelessness," according to Elizabeth Smith, a psychiatrist at Washington University in St. Louis, who has done extensive research on the psychological toll that disasters take on victims.

Curiously, however, as midwesterners slogged through the floodwaters, many showed remarkable resilience and good cheer, often using humor to relieve the misery. Others found it easier to cope if they could literally escape, even for short periods of time. As one volunteer psychologist in St. Louis, Illinois, noted, "You have to get away from it and see something

besides destruction and desperation." As in Vietnam, the possibility of even a temporary break in the stress seemed to play an important role in preventing burnout.

Wars and natural disasters are rare occurrences in the lives of most people, but virtually everyone is subject to the rigors of everyday stress. Parents who feel trapped by the endless needs of their small children, workers caught in the nine-to-five grind of high-pressure jobs—these people are no less subject to burnout than a soldier in the jungle. Unrelieved stress, regardless of its source, can ultimately lead to physical and mental breakdown. For example, the incidence of such symptoms as hypertension and stomach ulcers is unusually high among air-traffic controllers, a notoriously stressful occupation.

Yet even in such obviously stressful jobs, some individuals manage to avoid the negative consequences, and a few even thrive on the pressure. The key to whether someone will sink or swim seems to lie in attitude. "Each person learns to see the world through 'stress-colored glasses,' " note Robert L. Veninga and James P. Spradley in their 1981 book *The Work/Stress Connection*. "But the character of the

lens differs for each of us, so that an event that brings intense, unrelieved stress for one individual may affect another in only minor ways."

According to Veninga and Spradley, people who perceive greater stress will reach burnout more quickly, while those who are more tolerant of stress or who see it as a challenge run less risk. Because the fight-or-flight response is activated only when a threat is perceived, attitude is, in a sense, all. If focusing on the potentially threatening aspects of every situation can tend to do more harm than good, the better strategy is to learn to draw distinctions between real dangers and mere annoyances and worries.

Scientists studying the phenomenon of stress have discovered a number of so-called safety valves that can significantly reduce the negative repercussions of prolonged exposure to a stressor. One of the simplest and most effective of these safety valves is regular exercise. The concept is nothing new. More than 2,000 years ago, the Greek philosopher Plato wrote of the benefits of physical activity, noting that it was as important to exercise the body as the mind, in order to "preserve an equal and healthy balance between them." Indeed, modern studies have revealed that regular exercise does more than improve the body. In 1976 University of Wisconsin psychiatrist John Greist randomly divided 13 men and 15 women suffering from clinical depression into three groups, two of which received different forms of psychotherapy, while the third began a program of regular jogging without therapy. After 10 weeks, the runners showed just as much improvement as those who had received therapy. One 28-year-old jogger, dubbed Ms. X, improved dramatically for the first five weeks. But when an injured ankle forced her to stop, her depression returned. Three weeks later, when she resumed running, her depression again vanished. "I'm out of shape," she told the researchers, "but I know I'll get back in shape again." There could be no clearer indication that she had achieved a more positive outlook on life.

As promising as these results seemed, Greist himself acknowledged that a single experiment did not make scientific fact. Even if running had conferred psychological benefits on his patients, there might still be limits to what could be achieved through simple exercise. During the 1980s, nine different studies conducted in the United States and Canada tried to establish the relationship between physical fitness and the ability to cope with stress. Six of the experi-

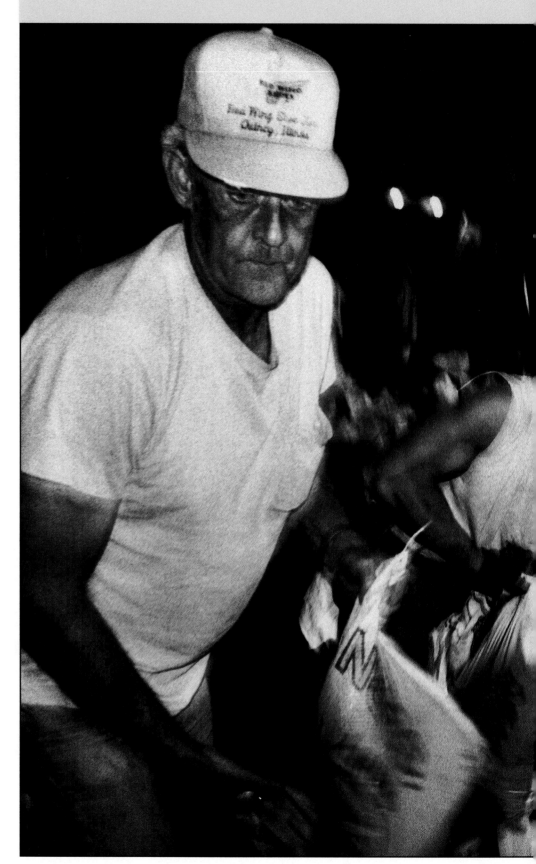

ments suggested that exercise programs have a positive effect on relieving stress, two showed mixed results, and one revealed no connection at all. In this last, performed in 1987, Canadian researchers put six previously sedentary volunteers through an intensive program of aerobic training. At the same time, measurements were taken of the volunteers' reactions to various stress tests, such as performing mental arithmetic while being exposed to white noise. After 10 weeks, the subjects' fitness level had improved, but there was no difference in their ability to deal with stress.

Other tests, however, offer persuasive evidence that a sense of control over one's plight can offset the effects of stress. In a now classic experiment whose results were published in 1983, researchers at the University of Denver and the University of Colorado at Boulder subjected rats in one group to a series of shocks that could be terminated when the animal pressed a bar. A second group of rats received equivalent shocks but had no means of controlling them, and a third group received no shocks. The scientists analyzed blood samples of the rats after the experiment to study the proliferation of certain disease-fighting cells,

Plunging down Rainbow Falls on California's Tuolumne River in a kayak can be a risky—even deadly—stunt. But even though some people might prefer more-tranquil modes of relaxation, many pursue such life-threatening activities as a means of relieving stress.

whose numbers have been shown to decline as a result of stress. The blood tests revealed that the immune systems of those rats unable to control the jolts were suppressed. By contrast, the immune systems of the rats that could halt the shocks were as sound as those of the rodents that had received no shocks at all. Similar experiments have shown that rats allowed to terminate shocks by turning a wheel developed stomach ulcers and other signs of stress more slowly than those that had no such control.

These animal tests confirmed an earlier study on humans. In 1969 researchers at the State University of New York at Stony Brook created stress in human subjects by exposing them to nine-second bursts of a loud noise. Those who had no way of controlling the random blasts made fewer attempts to solve an unsolvable puzzle and made more errors on a proofreading test than others who could shut off the sound with a switch.

Outside the laboratory, scientists have found a similar link between a sense of control and the perception of stress. Surveys conducted in various organizations, for example, reveal that middle-management personnel suffer from greater stress than people in top management. This, researchers believe, is because midlevel people have only limited control over circumstances, whereas those at the top

have the authority to change their situation. A sense of mastery over one's destiny thus seems crucial to alleviating the stress response. As researchers have also found, even those who are not actually in control but who have the illusion of control respond more positively to stress than those who believe they are powerless.

When it comes to a desire for control, however, the effects are not quite as clear cut. For example, studies of 41 undergraduate students conducted in the mid-1980s by Jerry M. Burger, a psychologist at Santa Clara University in California, reveal intriguing differences between the stress responses of people with a high desire for control and those with a low desire for control. Burger's assumption was that those eager to achieve control would generally be more anxious and thus impose on themselves greater levels of stress. Not surprisingly, however, the degree to which control could actually be achieved had a strong influence. Burger found, for example, that individuals with a high desire for control fared better than their counterparts when they were able to take an active, "hands-on" approach to the stressful situations. When the opportunity was presented to them, they

adopted more-aggressive coping strategies that appeared to reduce the overall level of stress.

On the other hand, faced with situations that were inherently uncontrollable, people who felt compelled to master a stressful situation were less able to cope than those with no such burning need. When it comes to handling stress, a high desire for control can be a "two-edged sword," as Burger has put it. If control is impossible, such as during a natural disaster, people who feel less desire to hold sway may in fact deal more effectively with the circumstances.

The rigors of everyday stress present challenges aplenty for most of us. Those such as parachutist Gregory Robertson who have managed to harness the power of the stress response to perform heroic acts represent special cases indeed. But in some instances, a failure to respond is so extraordinary, and so foreign to what we expect of our fellow human beings, that it raises questions of its own.

In 1964 a young woman named Kitty Genovese was stabbed to death in a residential section of Queens, in New York City. During the initial stages of the attack outside an apartment building, no fewer than 38 of her neighbors watched and listened to her cries for help—and did nothing. The incident shocked the nation and

prompted a flurry of psychological studies of what has come to be known as "the bystander effect."

In 1981 psychologists reported that in more than 55 experiments conducted by many different scientists under a variety of test conditions over the course of 13 years, lone bystanders offered help to victims of emergencies in 75 percent of the cases. When other people were present, however, the rate of intervention dropped to just 53 percent. The results indicate that the presence of others apparently diffuses the sense of personal responsibility and leads to the expectation that if help is necessary, someone else will provide it. However, statistics and scientific formulas do not always reflect reality: According to these experimental results, at least half of the nearly 40 witnesses to the Genovese murder should have come to her aid. As it was, not a single one did so.

Other research suggests that people who intervene in emergencies do indeed have special qualities that distinguish them from the average individual. They often have a high degree of self-assurance and feel that they can handle such situations by themselves. They may also have a need for self-esteem that outweighs any concerns for personal safety. In many cases, they are people with specialized training who, like Gregory Robertson, have the skills necessary to cope with

a given circumstance. But the same investigations have also revealed that a significant number of those who intervene are otherwise ordinary people who do not view themselves as heroes but who somehow—in ways they can rarely articulate—were able to tap into internal resources that spurred their heroism.

During World War II, a small percentage of non-Jewish Europeans risked their own lives to provide food, clothing, shelter, and encouragement for their Jewish neighbors fleeing the Holocaust. Studies conducted after the war divide these brave souls into two broad categories: people who were motivated by deeply held moral values, and those who acted for personal and emotional reasons. Interestingly, men tended to belong to the first group, women to the second.

It would be tempting to conclude that people with strong religious beliefs are more likely to help others in distress than are those without such convictions. But numerous studies conducted from the 1950s through the 1990s have shown this not to be the case. Some of the most convincing evidence comes from a study by Samuel and Pearl Oliner, husband-and-wife researchers at Humboldt State University in Arcata, California. They performed a painstaking examination of the motivations of non-Jewish residents who had rescued Jews during World War II—people like the peasant woman who shielded Samuel Oliner himself, then 12 years old, from the Nazis after his family was murdered.

In the course of their research, the Oliners interviewed hundreds of people who had lived in Poland, France, Germany, the Netherlands, and Italy at the time of the German occupation. The couple wanted to learn, among other things, what role religion played in distinguishing the rescuers from those they called the nonrescuers, people who did not help. As the Oliners noted in their 1988 book, *The Altruistic Personality*, "rescuers did not differ significantly from bystanders or nonrescuers with respect to their religious identification, religious education, and their own religiosity or that of their parents." Their research also revealed that "one's identification with a religious body does not ensure that one will endorse values of tolerance and brotherhood."

Other studies point to the same conclusion. In one 1973 experiment, for instance, Princeton University psychologists John M. Darley and C. Daniel Batson determined that religious beliefs have little bearing on altruistic behavior—particularly if the would-be helper is in a hurry. As part

The Simple Valor of Doing Right

During the years of terror that followed the Nazi invasion of Holland in 1940, German troops in Amsterdam descended time and again on the old schoolhouse that Tina Strobos, a young medical student, shared with her mother. The soldiers spent hours pounding on walls and ripping up carpets in their search for Jews in hiding. But after eight such raids, the Nazis had found nothing.

Strobos and her mother, alerted to each impending raid by an informant at Gestapo headquarters, managed to keep the soldiers from discovering a secret room they had built in their home. Although the tiny hideout could hold no more than two people at a time, over the years it provided safe haven to a stream of nearly 100 refugees. Among them was Tirzah van Amerongen, who appears with Strobos (*far right*) in this series of photographs from 1940.

Strobos, now a psychiatrist, risked her own life to save the lives of others, many of them strangers. She remains proud of her actions but shuns adulation, saying that she simply wants to be "counted as one of the good guys."

of the experiment, the researchers assembled a group of students in one building, then asked them to walk over to another building where technicians were waiting to record their comments on a prearranged topic. Some of the students were told that they were late and had been expected at the other building a few minutes earlier. As the unsuspecting students passed through an alley, they encountered a shabbily dressed man slumped in a doorway, coughing and groaning. The students who had been instilled with a sense of urgency were more likely to ignore the "victim," who had been planted there as part of the experiment. Some even stepped over him on their way. More surprising still, these were students from Princeton Theological Seminary, and the topic they were going to talk about was the parable of the good Samaritan.

The grim view of human nature painted by such instances of the "bystander effect" is somewhat brightened by evidence that most people possess a streak of altruism. "Even in our society," in the words of New York University psychologist Martin Hoffman, "the evidence is overwhelming that most people, when confronted with someone in a distress situation, will make a move to help very quickly if circumstances permit." That altruistic streak seems to be most evident in people from small towns. In one study

conducted in several U.S. towns and cities, researchers watched the reactions of passersby to the anguished pleas of a young child standing, as part of the experiment, on a sidewalk. "I'm lost," the child told them. "Can you call my house?" Almost three-quarters of the adults in small towns offered assistance, but fewer than half of those in big cities did so.

In city and town alike, however, the urge to help others appears to be a fundamental element of the human psyche, a trait that seems to arise at quite an early age. Observations of infants as young as 10 to 14 months have shown responses to the pain of others that represent at least the foundations of altruism. In their second year, children may even offer direct comfort, such as patting the head of someone who seems to be in pain. Researchers in one study videotaped 30 hours of free play by more than two dozen three- to five-year-olds, and the footage revealed some 1,200 acts of sharing, helping, and cooperation. Of course, children also have a dark, selfish side, which may often seem to overshadow any generosity of spirit. But as a number of studies suggest, inklings of a certain sensitivity are evident even in newborns, who

have been shown to wail more intensely at another baby's cry than at other equally shrill noises. While this reaction does not necessarily represent empathy, claims Hoffman, "it is evidence of a primitive precursor to it. There's a basic human tendency to be responsive to other persons' needs, not just your own."

So far, however, this tendency—this invisible, unquantifiable predisposition toward goodwill—has eluded the exacting instruments of science. That some people are willing to risk life and limb for others, blatantly flouting nature's laws of self-preservation, ultimately cannot be laid to mere hormones or the cold chemistry of the general adaptation syndrome. The impulse defies our common physiology, arising not from cells and tissue but from flickers in that remote corner of the mind where thoughts are informed by memories and emotion. Efforts to understand human response have yielded vivid maps of the body's physical landscape but only shadows of the force that animates it. This much is clear: At times of crisis, each one of us has the choice of helping or merely watching, of engaging the powers within or risking being virtually paralyzed by them. In the end, it is the decision to act, more than the actions themselves, that defines the hero and tips the ordinary into the realm of the extraordinary.

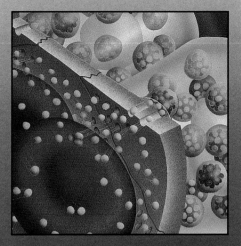

THE STRESS RESPONSE: MARSHALING MIND AND BODY

The body reacts instantly to any sensation of threat, whether a pop quiz at school or a piercing scream in the middle of the night. Regardless of the stimulus, the stress response—a chain reaction of self-protective measures—radiates through the nervous system and the endocrine system, sparking more than 1,400 physiochemical reactions that in turn produce sometimes dramatic changes everywhere in the body.

Sources of stress vary from person to person. Just as the distinction between friend and foe is subjective, so is one's notion of stress, which depends largely on emotion, experience, and individual perception. Some people are overcome with fear at the sight of a dog, for example, while others feel only affection. The perception of stress can also change over time: A toddler who jumps in fright the first time she sees the neighbor's retriever might become less afraid after several encounters and eventually tug playfully on the animal's tail.

External stimuli are not the only possible stressors; the body employs the same physical and chemical reactions to deal with perils conjured by the mind or with such internal threats as viral infection or other disease. This common response to stress, known as the general adaptation syndrome, was first identified by endocrinologist Hans Selye in the 1930s. Selye outlined three stages in the body's stress response: alarm, resistance, and exhaustion. If the stress continues for long periods without relief or is so great that it overwhelms the defenses, according to Selye, exhaustion can even lead to death.

Nevertheless, the stress response plays an essential role in helping the body to react quickly and decisively to sudden threatening changes in its environment. And when the threats recede, the body uses similar mechanisms in order to return to its normal state of homeostasis—a steady level of functioning amidst the ordinary fluctuations of life.

AN EARLY-WARNING SYSTEM

The stress response depends on the interplay of two major nerve networks. Sensory nerves of the peripheral nervous system relay signals to the spinal cord and brain, vital partners in the central nervous system. If the brain interprets the impulses as a threat, it instructs the autonomic division of the peripheral nervous system to act.

The autonomic network—which controls the involuntary functions of certain muscles and organs, including the heart—is itself divided into two branches. The sympathetic branch mobilizes the body's energy and resources for high performance; the parasympathetic branch helps slow down and restore the body's systems in the aftermath of the threat. These contrary functions combine to keep the body operating normally.

Seconds after a stressor is detected, the sympathetic division goes into action, firing off messages through its network of neurons. From the brain, impulses travel down the spinal cord and out to nearby ganglia—nerve cell clusters, arranged like links in a microscopic chain. The ganglia serve as information hubs, broadcasting to various tissues and organs by way of myriad fibers. When the threat recedes, the parasympathetic system takes over, sending impulses through its own fibers from the spinal cord to more distant ganglionic hubs.

AUTONOMIC NERVOUS SYSTEM. An intricate network of fibers carries signals from the brain to various parts of the body *(right)*. The autonomic system's sympathetic division *(purple)* extends through thoracic and lumbar nerves along the spinal cord to chains of ganglia, and from there to target organs and tissues. Longer parasympathetic fibers *(green)* emerge from cranial and sacral nerves and connect to ganglia that lie near or within target areas.

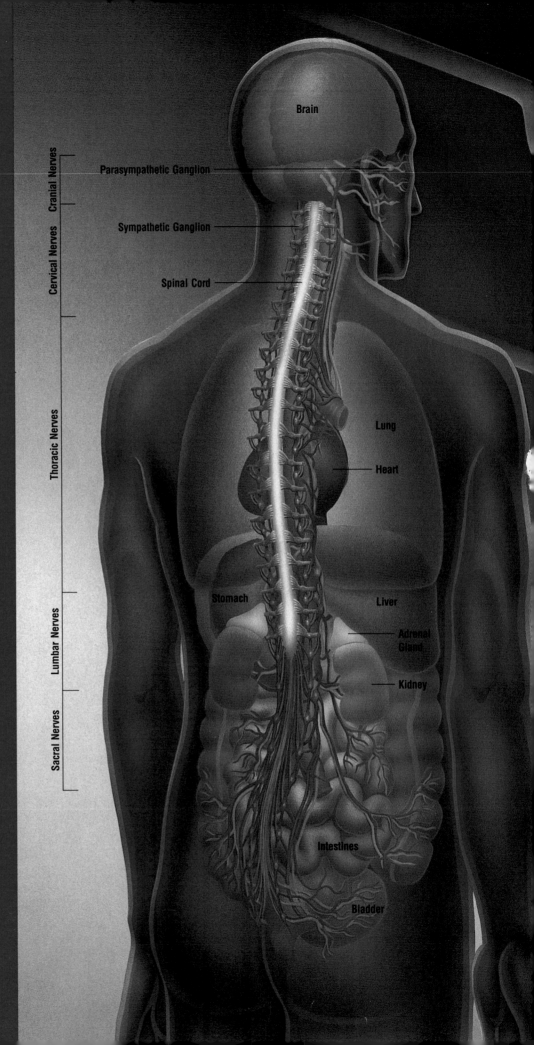

Brain

Cranial Nerves

Parasympathetic Ganglion

Cervical Nerves

Sympathetic Ganglion

Spinal Cord

Thoracic Nerves

Lung

Heart

Stomach

Liver

Lumbar Nerves

Adrenal Gland

Kidney

Sacral Nerves

Intestines

Bladder

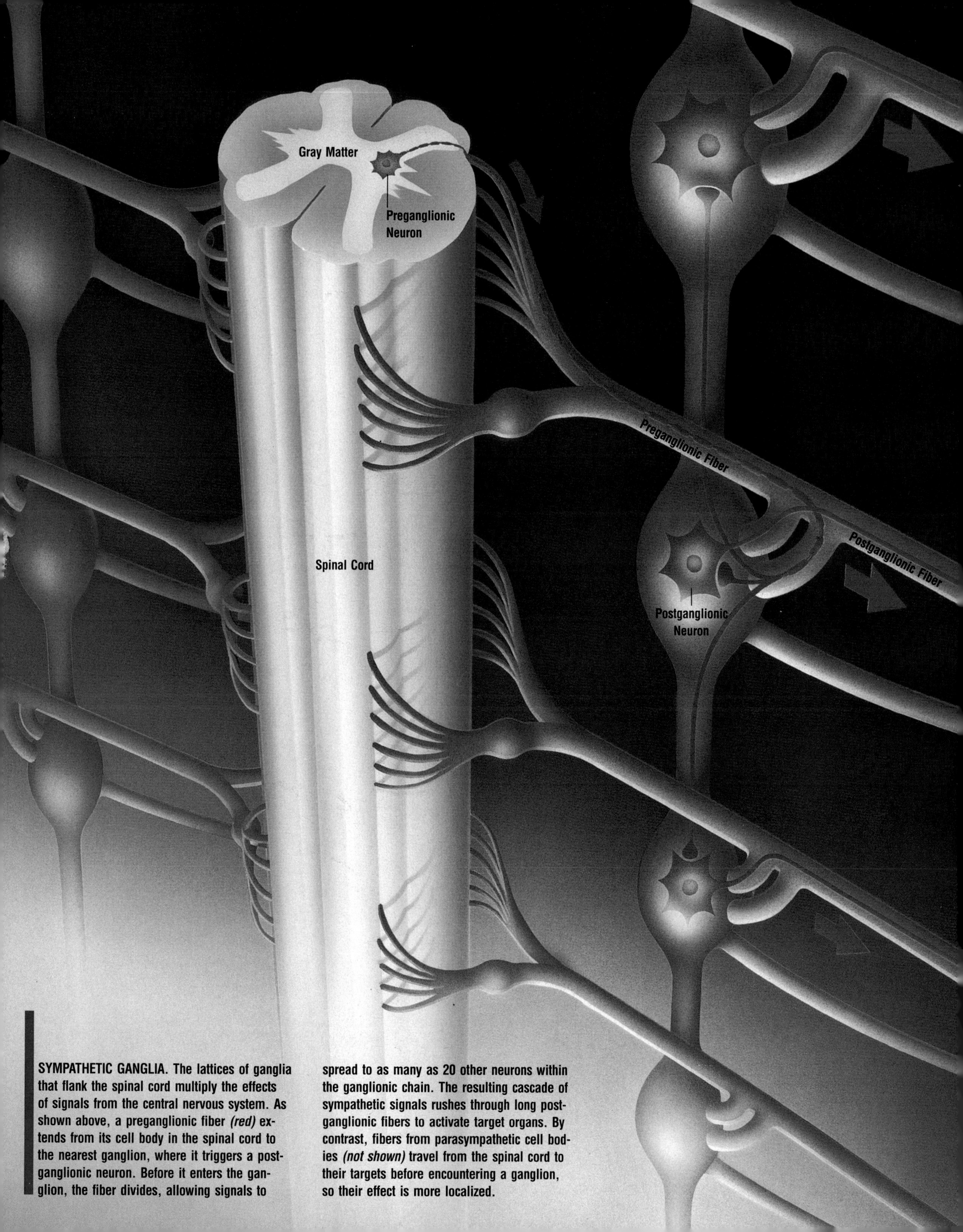

Gray Matter

Preganglionic Neuron

Spinal Cord

Preganglionic Fiber

Postganglionic Fiber

Postganglionic Neuron

SYMPATHETIC GANGLIA. The lattices of ganglia that flank the spinal cord multiply the effects of signals from the central nervous system. As shown above, a preganglionic fiber *(red)* extends from its cell body in the spinal cord to the nearest ganglion, where it triggers a postganglionic neuron. Before it enters the ganglion, the fiber divides, allowing signals to spread to as many as 20 other neurons within the ganglionic chain. The resulting cascade of sympathetic signals rushes through long postganglionic fibers to activate target organs. By contrast, fibers from parasympathetic cell bodies *(not shown)* travel from the spinal cord to their targets before encountering a ganglion, so their effect is more localized.

38

THE ALARM TO FIGHT OR FLEE

Alerted to the presence of a threat, the brain's higher centers pass the message along to several key structures. Chief among these is the hypothalamus, which activates the first level of the stress response, known as the alarm stage.

Nerve impulses surge through the sympathetic branch to various organs of the chest and abdomen, all of which play crucial roles in meeting the challenge: The heart (*right*) begins to pump harder and faster; the lungs also pick up the pace to bring in more oxygen. Meanwhile, the digestive tract—its functions less necessary for immediate survival—reduces its activity to a minimum.

Other parts of the body also respond to the alarm. Pupils dilate in order to capture more light, sweat breaks out on the surface of the skin to cool off the body, and dilated vessels increase the blood flow to skeletal muscles, making them stronger.

Within seconds, the body is prepared to perform at its highest possible levels, either to fight the threat or to flee to safety. The effects of this high alert last only a few seconds, however, so if the threat persists, the body must take further measures.

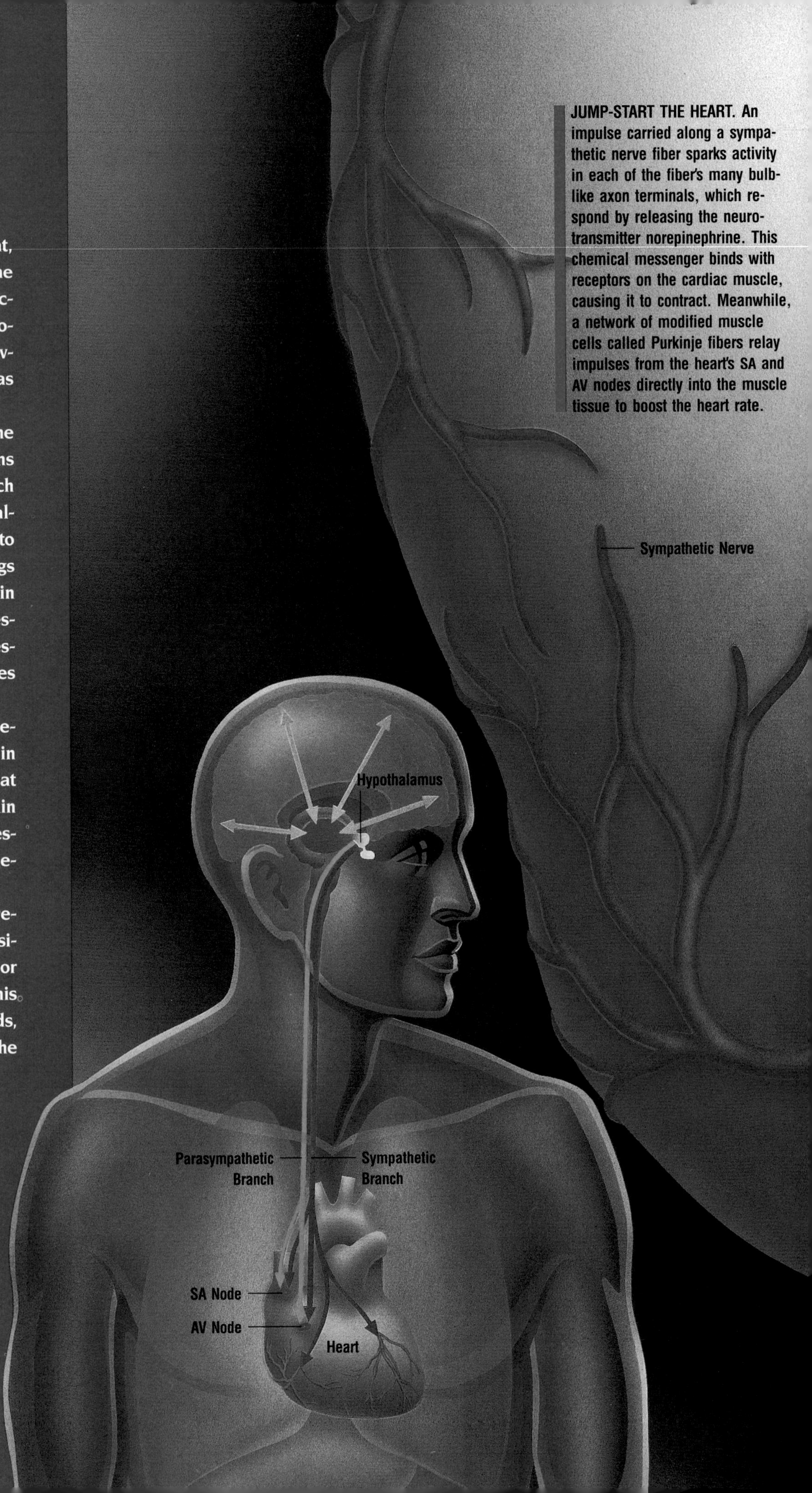

ROUTES TO THE HEART. The figure at right shows potential pathways for impulses to travel from the hypothalamus to the heart. During the stress response, sympathetic signals travel directly into the cardiac muscle to increase the force of contraction, and into the SA and AV nodes—cardiac fibers that act as natural pacemakers—to speed the heart rate. Later, parasympathetic signals instruct the nodes to slow down the pace.

JUMP-START THE HEART. An impulse carried along a sympathetic nerve fiber sparks activity in each of the fiber's many bulb-like axon terminals, which respond by releasing the neurotransmitter norepinephrine. This chemical messenger binds with receptors on the cardiac muscle, causing it to contract. Meanwhile, a network of modified muscle cells called Purkinje fibers relay impulses from the heart's SA and AV nodes directly into the muscle tissue to boost the heart rate.

Sympathetic Nerve

Hypothalamus

Parasympathetic Branch — Sympathetic Branch

SA Node

AV Node

Heart

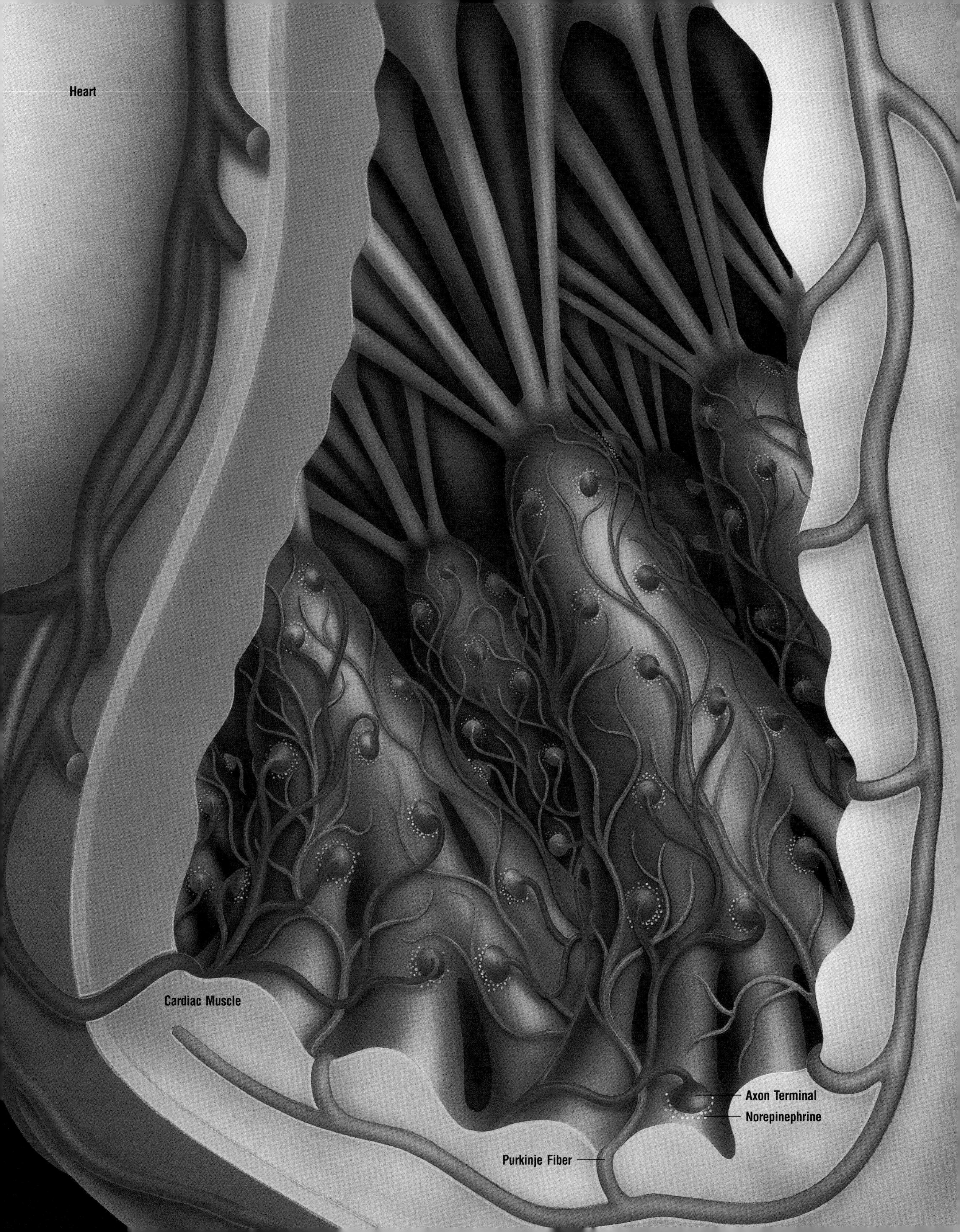

Heart

Cardiac Muscle

Axon Terminal

Norepinephrine

Purkinje Fiber

MAINTAINING THE INITIAL RESPONSE

The nervous system can keep up the body's stress response only for a short time—just long enough for the endocrine system to swing into action. The glands of this system, also under the direction of the hypothalamus, send messages throughout the body by secreting substances called hormones into the bloodstream. Although some hormones are chemically the same as neurotransmitters, their effects develop more slowly and last longer.

Stimulated by the same neural activity that provokes the body's initial reactions, the adrenal glands, located just above the kidneys, release two kinds of hormones, epinephrine and norepinephrine. These two chemicals, borne by the circulating blood, bind with specialized receptors on target organs, where they trigger specific activities. In the heart, for example, epinephrine maintains the rapid heart rate already established by the nervous system, and norepinephrine increases blood pressure. Elsewhere in the body, the hormones stimulate breathing and inhibit digestion, allowing the body to maintain a high level of activity. The clearest sign of this adrenal activity comes in the seconds after a sudden fright, as the knees shake, the teeth chatter, and the heart pounds.

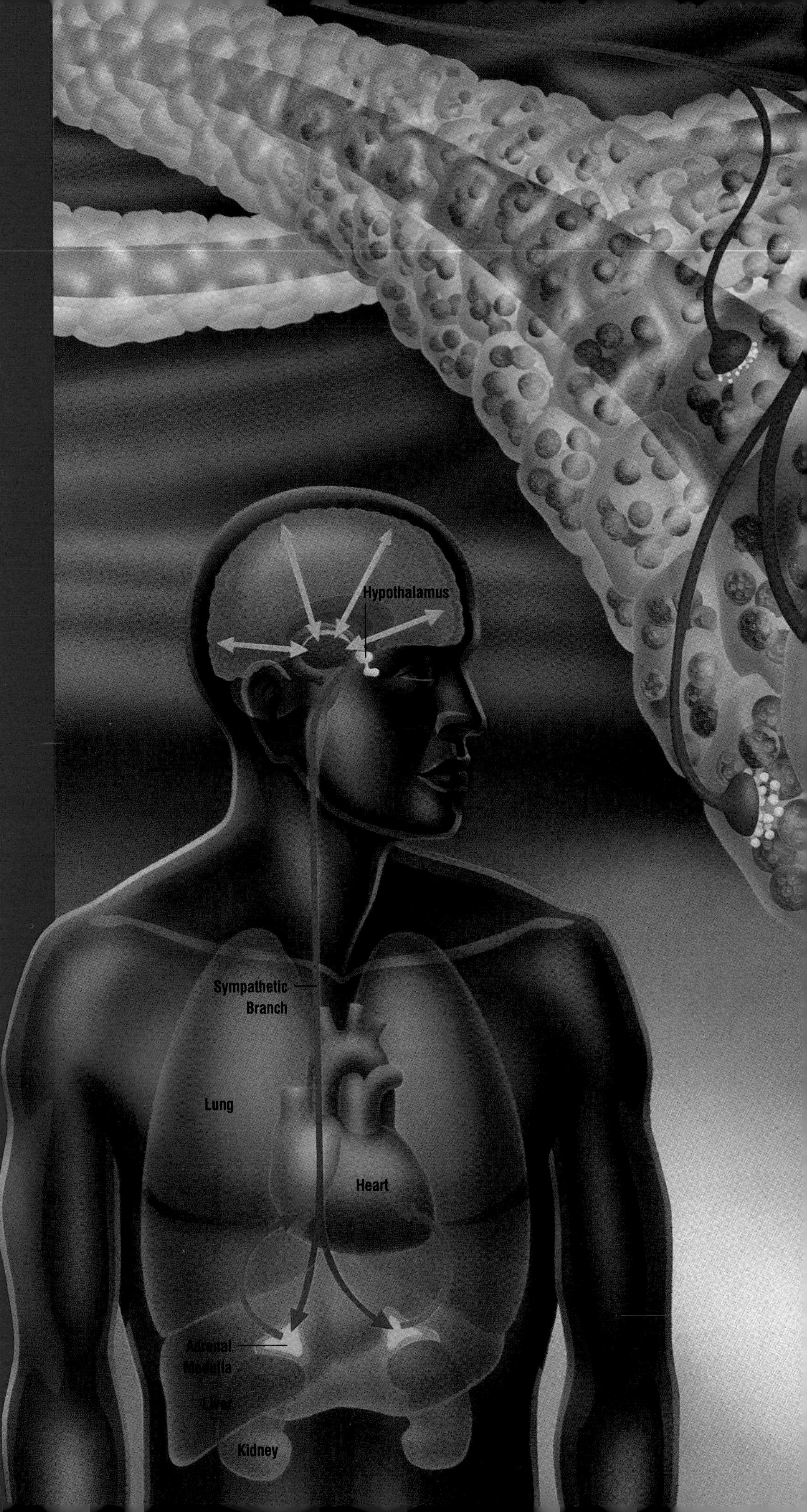

ADRENAL MEDULLAS. The endocrine system's involvement in the stress reaction begins when messengers of the initial alert reach the adrenal glands, as shown in the figure at right. Impulses carried along fibers of the sympathetic nervous system penetrate to the core, or medulla, of each adrenal gland. The medullas, in turn, respond by secreting hormones that circulate to such organs as the heart, lungs, and liver.

Hypothalamus

Sympathetic Branch

Lung

Heart

Adrenal Medulla

Liver

Kidney

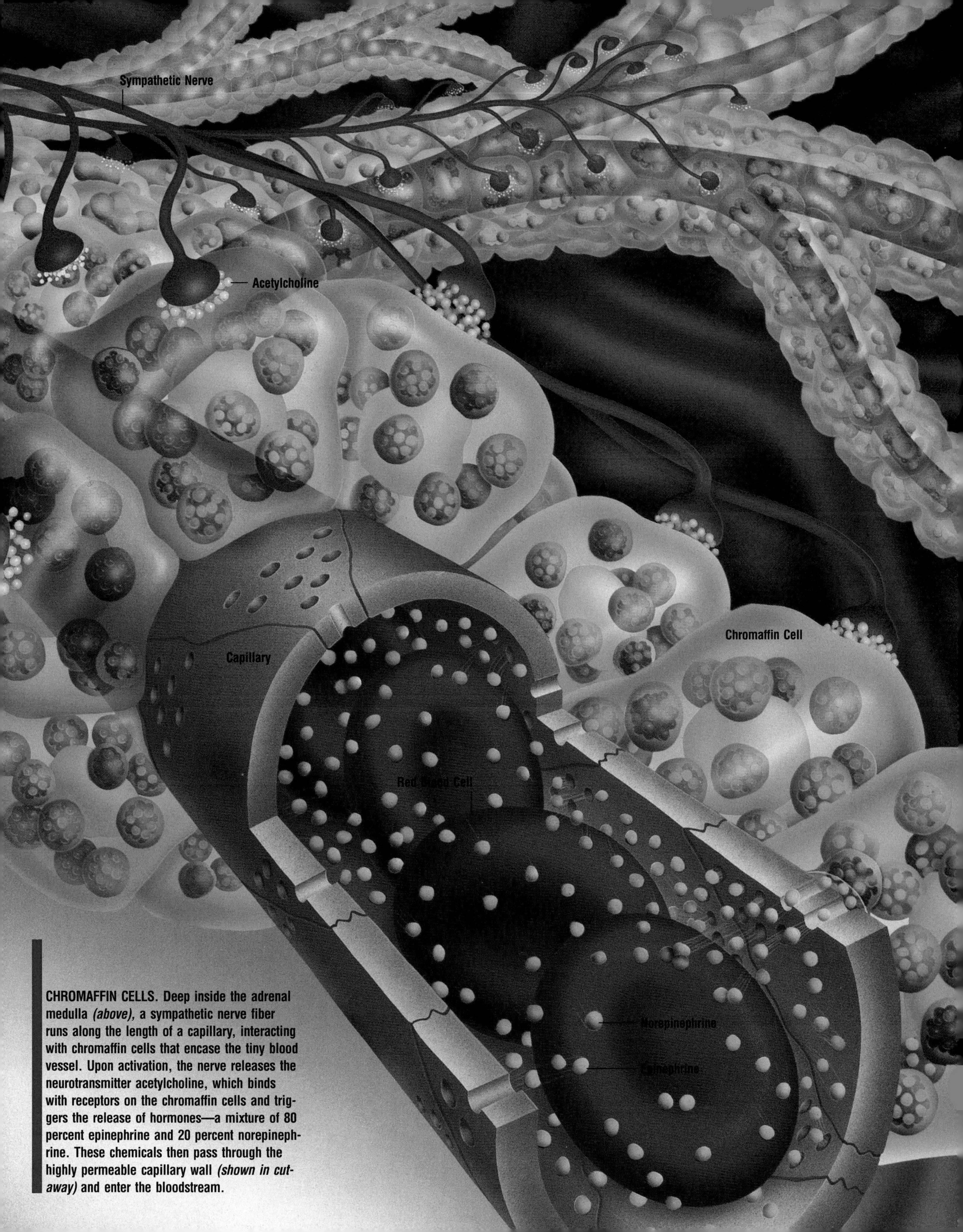

Sympathetic Nerve

Acetylcholine

Capillary

Chromaffin Cell

Red Blood Cell

Norepinephrine

Epinephrine

CHROMAFFIN CELLS. Deep inside the adrenal medulla *(above),* a sympathetic nerve fiber runs along the length of a capillary, interacting with chromaffin cells that encase the tiny blood vessel. Upon activation, the nerve releases the neurotransmitter acetylcholine, which binds with receptors on the chromaffin cells and triggers the release of hormones—a mixture of 80 percent epinephrine and 20 percent norepinephrine. These chemicals then pass through the highly permeable capillary wall *(shown in cutaway)* and enter the bloodstream.

HORMONES TO KEEP UP THE RESISTANCE

If the threat persists beyond the burst of activity generated during the alarm reaction, the next phase of the stress response, resistance, kicks in. During this stage, the hypothalamus orchestrates a cascade of hormones that prepares the body for a more sustained response.

On orders from the hypothalamus, the nearby pituitary gland releases its own hormones, which in turn circulate to other glands throughout the body. Those glands release still more hormones bound for numerous target organs. For example, the outer portion, or cortex, of each adrenal gland secretes cortisol, a key chemical messenger linked to acute and chronic stress. This hormone increases the supply of blood glucose, particularly for the brain and heart, and helps turn fat into energy. To focus that energy against the threat, cortisol also depresses the reproductive and immune systems and other functions that make no immediate contribution.

The effort to keep key organs functioning at maximum efficiency can exact a significant toll. If the threat is not overcome during the resistance stage, the body's reserves begin to dwindle, ushering in the final phase of the stress response, exhaustion.

ENDOCRINE RESISTANCE. Taking its cue from the hypothalamus, as shown in the figure at right, the pituitary gland secretes hormones that spur the adrenal cortices to release chemicals of their own. The resulting mix of bloodborne hormones acts on tissue such as skeletal muscle, causing protein breakdown and transport of amino acids to the liver, where they are converted into energy.

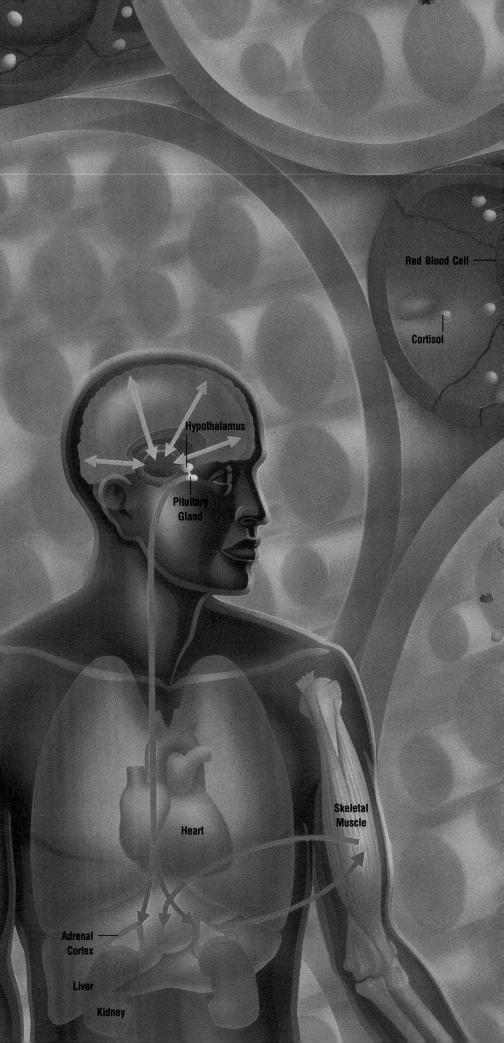

Red Blood Cell

Cortisol

Hypothalamus

Pituitary Gland

Skeletal Muscle

Heart

Adrenal Cortex

Liver

Kidney

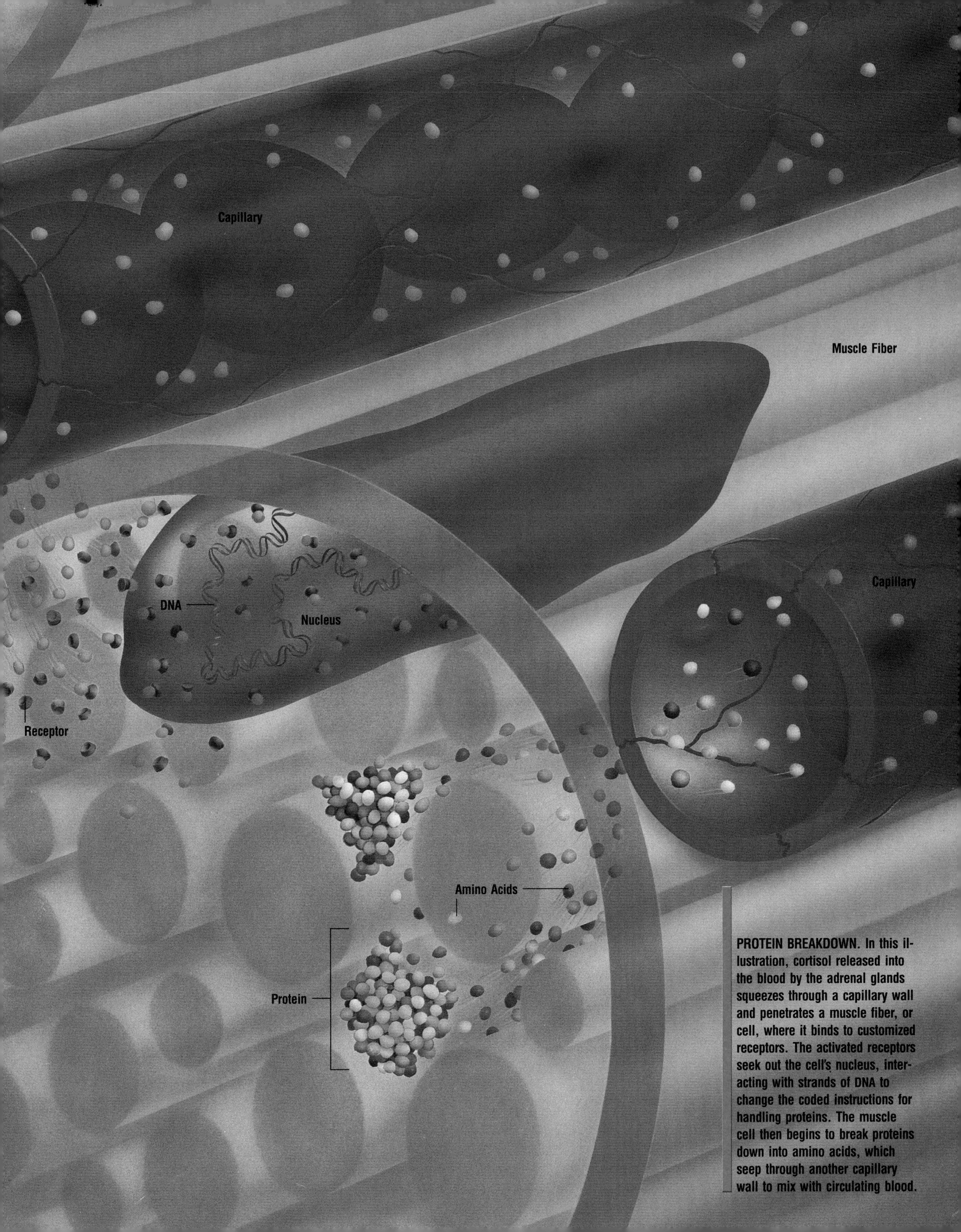

Capillary

Muscle Fiber

DNA

Nucleus

Capillary

Receptor

Amino Acids

Protein

PROTEIN BREAKDOWN. In this illustration, cortisol released into the blood by the adrenal glands squeezes through a capillary wall and penetrates a muscle fiber, or cell, where it binds to customized receptors. The activated receptors seek out the cell's nucleus, interacting with strands of DNA to change the coded instructions for handling proteins. The muscle cell then begins to break proteins down into amino acids, which seep through another capillary wall to mix with circulating blood.

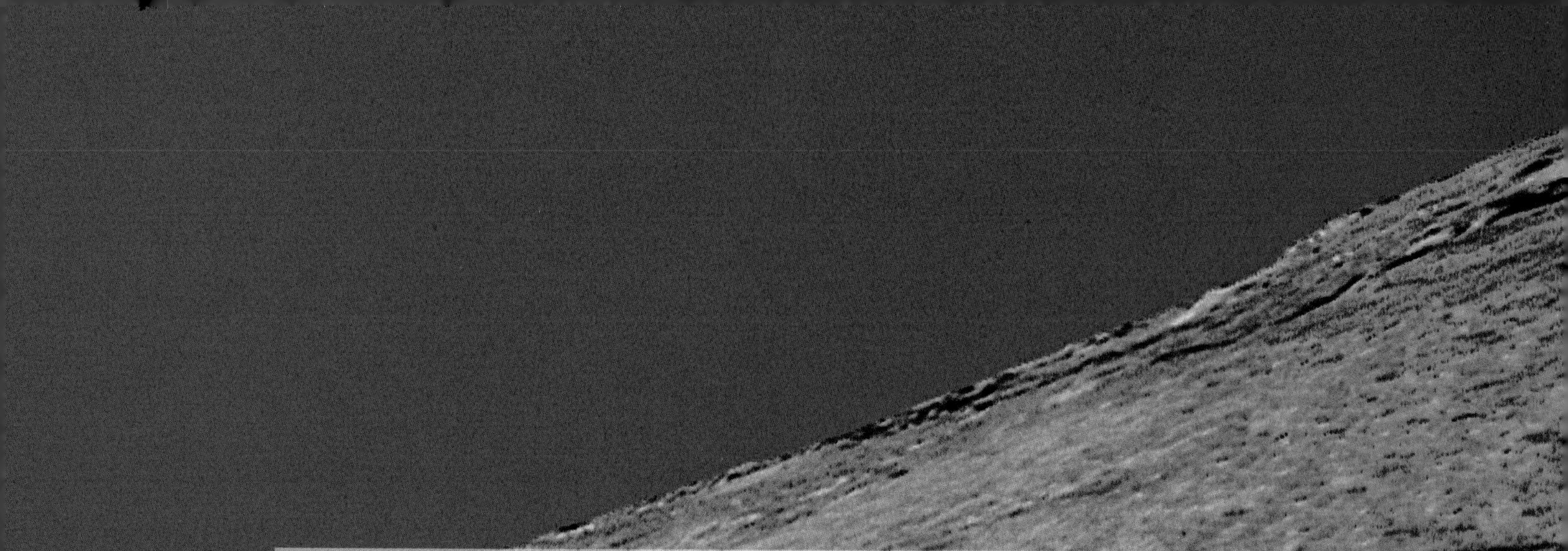

2
Power to Endure

For many people, a brush with death can leave behind a life-diminishing legacy of fear. But for a college student and mountain climber named Rob Schultheis, confronting his own mortality left him more profoundly alive than he had ever thought possible.

One dusty June morning in 1964, during his summer vacation, Schultheis set out from Boulder, Colorado, hitchhiking along a road through canyons and forest toward the Rocky Mountains' Front Range. By late afternoon, having reached the end of the road, Schultheis set up camp at an old mining shack near a creek. The shack was several thousand feet up in the high country, and he spent the frigid night shivering in his army-surplus sleeping bag.

The next morning Schultheis started off again, aiming to reach the top of 12,814-foot Mount Neva. The trail carried him across fields of broken rock, or scree, and into hard-packed snow six feet deep in some places. A relative newcomer to the intricacies of technical rock climbing, he traversed steep inclines where he had to chop toeholds out of the snow with his ice ax and steady himself with spiked crampons strapped to the soles of his boots. In time he made it to a series of rocky ledges and from there, forcing himself to climb despite a bout of vertigo, onto the mountain's summit.

Atop Neva, Schultheis had only a few minutes to savor his triumph. What had started out as a glorious midsummer sky had now turned ominous: Thunder rumbled across the valley below, and wind-swept hail pelted him. Consulting his topographic map, he decided to head down by what looked to be a more direct—if more difficult—route.

"Anyone in his right mind, with a grain of sense, would have turned and gone down the same way he had come up," Schultheis wrote in his 1986 book, *Bone Games*. "But I was not in my right mind that day; I had left logic far behind." Instead—"possessed by something between panic and euphoria, dread and ecstasy"—he struck out along Neva's ridge line.

The ridge soon narrowed, until he was flanked by precipitous drops that only an expert should have attempted. The novice pressed onward. Finally, spying what looked to be a way off the crest, Schultheis lowered himself from an overhang into a crevice. But midway down the rockface, hanging by his fingers from a knobby spur, he found himself unable to find a toehold. Retreat was out of the question: He had neither the skill nor the strength to haul his weight up from a full extension. "I hung there for I don't know how long: 30 seconds, two min-

utes, half an hour," Schultheis recalled. "The blood drained from my arms; my fingers went dead. Finally, without meaning to, I let go."

As he fell, he bounced repeatedly off the mountainside, slamming again and again into the ice ax and sharp-pointed crampons he had slung over his shoulder. "Suddenly it all stopped: I was lying on a narrow, sloping ledge; my head lay next to the emptiness, and I was staring down into at least 200 feet of thin air."

Schultheis's legs were bloody and his back punctured in dozens of places. Hurt and terrified, he lay

there weeping. With no shelter, no food or water, he knew he would die of exposure once nightfall came. Survival required one thing: that he make it back to camp. It took "a long, long time," he wrote, "but slowly, painfully, I put together the elaborate series of moves that got me up on my knees." From his knees he made it to his feet and then started down the mountain.

Once he started walking, he found that—by some magic—his pain had vanished, his fear evaporated. He had entered a state of heightened awareness where his vision was acute, his sense of touch and balance sharp. Unmindful that death dogged his every move, he was euphorically aware of "the brilliant crystals in the granite, the drunken calligraphy of ice crys-

North Dakota farm boy John Thompson jokes with friends, a pair of splints the only visible evidence of an accident five months earlier in which a grain machine rotor tore off both his arms. Despite terrible pain, Thompson had the presence of mind to call for help on a push-button phone, using a pen clenched in his teeth. Even though he had lost half his blood by the time the medics arrived, he was able to remind them to gather up his severed arms, which surgeons were later able to reattach.

tals." On one 15-foot, sheer vertical face, he seemed to cling to the very grain of the rock. Some of the moves he was making were far beyond his skills—"a dance in which a single missed beat would have been fatal"— but he seemed to have gained the surefootedness of a mountain goat.

Even though some part of him was afraid and exhausted, Schultheis was filled with an overwhelming sense of joy at being alive. He shinnied down a pillar of ice, leaped from perch to perch with "no regrets, no hesitation," he wrote. "There were no false moves left in me. I couldn't miss because

there was no such thing as a miss. It didn't matter whether I fell or not, because I could not fall, any more than two plus two can equal three. It was all sublime nonsense, of course, but I believed it, down in my very cells; if I hadn't believed, I would have been hurled into the Pit below."

Eventually, Schultheis stumbled back to the trail and down to the mining shack. The next morning, after another freezing night, he limped to the road and caught a ride into town. For two days he slept as though drugged, a man who had been drained of his wherewithal. But he had come to believe that on Mount Neva he had been filled with "a brand of grace" that had lifted him out of his everyday life into the realm of the gods.

Whatever happened to Rob Schultheis during his ordeal on the mountainside, it was an elusive experience, one that he has spent many years trying to recapture. This quest for a state of heightened awareness and physical exaltation is not new, nor is it limited to the realm of sport. Ancient Hindu and Buddhist texts, for instance, relate examples of amazing physical and mental prowess, as do anthropological descriptions of aboriginal peoples who undergo torturous rites of initiation—cutting off their own fingers, for instance, or piercing their flesh with skewers. Individuals in all of these traditions have been reputed to withstand extremes of pain and to perform extraordinary feats of endurance, strength, and agility.

Recognition by Western science that members of certain cultures do in fact have the ability to control autonomic functions at will—altering their blood pressure, skin temperature, and oxygen uptake, and radically inhibiting pain—has been somewhat belated. However, in the past 20 years or so, researchers have begun to explore the subject in earnest, with an eye toward developing clinical methods—from biofeedback to mental imaging and positive thinking—that would allow patients to marshal their own inner resources to similar effect.

One intriguing model for how human beings have learned to control their supposedly involuntary bodily systems is that of shamans (a word that probably derives from a central Asian language, from a noun meaning "one who knows"). Archaeologists interpreting clues found in elaborate cave paintings have proposed that shamanism may have existed some 16,000 years ago in southern France and northern Spain. The late American mythologist Joseph Campbell believed that shamanic practices spread from the western Mediterranean throughout Europe, Africa, and Asia and over the Bering land bridge down into North and South America.

According to Campbell, a shaman was "a particular type of medicine man," whose powers were believed to arise "from his intercourse with envisioned spirits." To confront these spirits, the shamans danced, chanted, or beat drums until they fell into trances or collapsed in fits. Such a person, Campbell wrote, was now able "to cause illness and to heal the sick, to communicate with the world beyond, to foresee the future, and to influence both the weather and the movements of game animals."

Campbell has suggested that by such rituals, ancient peoples threw themselves into a neurological state akin to dreaming or drug-induced hallucinations. Tradition holds that shamans—who still exist in some cultures—can withstand excessive heat and cold, sustain their energy without food or water, and manifest supernormal physical skill and strength. One famed shaman was Milarepa, a ninth-century Buddhist mystic and poet who wandered the high ranges of the Himalayas along the present-day Nepalese-Tibetan border. In this region of rarefied air and deadly cold, Milarepa is said to have worn only a thin cloth and to have eaten only nettle soup and roasted barley flour.

Milarepa's ability to survive the harsh mountain climate is attributed to a form of yoga called *tummo*, whose principal aim is to accept the intangibility of the body and thereby be freed from worldly distractions. As an adept of tummo, Milarepa could reputedly warm himself against frigid blasts by releasing so-called psychic heat. According to Tibetan texts, the ability is gained through meditation by visualizing burning suns in the middle of the palms of the hands, the soles of the feet, and an area just below the navel. (Indeed, researchers have seen naked tummo yogis sitting outside radiating enough heat to melt snow around them or rapidly dry wet sheets laid against their skin.)

Most shamans passed on their knowledge to young boys—and occasionally to girls—of their tribes through initiations that might take months. Surviving these rituals could in itself be an awesome task. In the 1830s, for instance, young men of the Mandan tribe of the Mississippi River valley underwent rites that required them to hang suspended from skewers threaded through their flesh. One explorer trekking across northern Canada in the 1920s met a shaman of the Inuit who told of his own initiation years earlier. He had been taken in the dead of winter to a remote spot and placed on an animal skin inside a tiny hut made of snow. For 30 days he

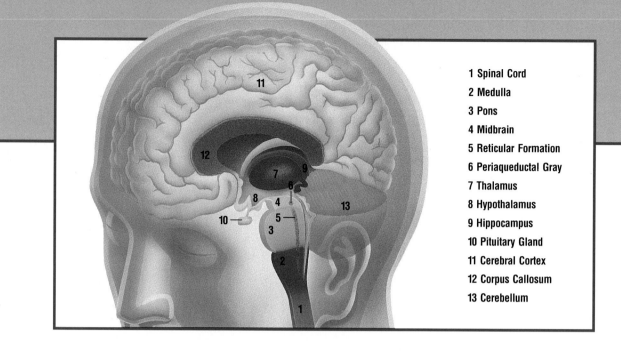

1 Spinal Cord
2 Medulla
3 Pons
4 Midbrain
5 Reticular Formation
6 Periaqueductal Gray
7 Thalamus
8 Hypothalamus
9 Hippocampus
10 Pituitary Gland
11 Cerebral Cortex
12 Corpus Callosum
13 Cerebellum

The Brain's Role in Pain

A person in pain—whether from a stubbed toe or a badly broken bone—typically assumes that the discomfort is a physical sensation, located in the injured tissue. Actually, the experience is as much mental as it is physical. Emotions and thoughts arising in the brain invariably shape the perception of pain, and, by a kind of neurochemical countermessaging, they can even curtail the flow of bad news from the body.

The pain-sensing process (*pages* 50-51) begins when injury to tissue in peripheral parts of the body causes specialized nerve endings called nociceptors to transmit impulses along pathways that terminate in layers of the soft, gray matter of the spine known as the dorsal horn. A switching junction of sorts, the dorsal horn sends the injury signals up the spinal cord to the brain by two basic routes. Some impulses move rapidly and directly to the thalamus, a relay structure deep in the brain that handles most kinds of sensory information; these fast-traveling signals seem to create the sensations we recognize as sharp pain. Other impulses, associated with diffuse types of pain, move more slowly and take a less-direct route to the thalamus. Within the brainstem—consisting of the medulla, pons, and midbrain—the impulses branch off to parts of a structure called the reticular formation. This mass of neurons runs the length of the brainstem and includes the periaqueductal gray, an area in the midbrain that, besides routing incoming nerve traffic to the thalamus, can send inhibiting messages back to the lower brainstem and spinal cord.

From the thalamus, neural pathways lead to the adjacent limbic system—a ring of structures, including the hypothalamus, associated with the emotions—and to parts of the cerebral cortex, which processes sensory information and is concerned with higher mental functions. As the fast- and slow-moving impulses reach the thalamus and pass to the limbic and cortical areas, the disturbance we describe as pain emerges.

The emotional aspect of the sensation is what we define as unpleasant, while rational and sensory interpretation of the impulses locates the sensation and identifies it as "aching," "stinging," or "burning." In turn, thoughts and emotions generated by the cerebral cortex and the limbic system can cause the periaqueductal gray to send neurotransmitters to the dorsal horn, prompting the release of morphinelike opioids (*pages* 58-59) and other chemical messengers that induce neurons to block impulses coming in from the nociceptors. The volume of signals actually reaching the limbic and cortical centers, rather than the number of impulses created at the site of the injury, determines how intensely the pain is felt.

Pathways in the Pain-Sensing System

1 Dorsal Horn
2 Medulla
3 Pons
4 Midbrain
5 Reticular Formation
6 Periaqueductal Gray
7 Thalamus
8 Hypothalamus
9 Hippocampus
10 Pituitary Gland
11 Cerebral Cortex
12 Corpus Callosum
13 Cerebellum

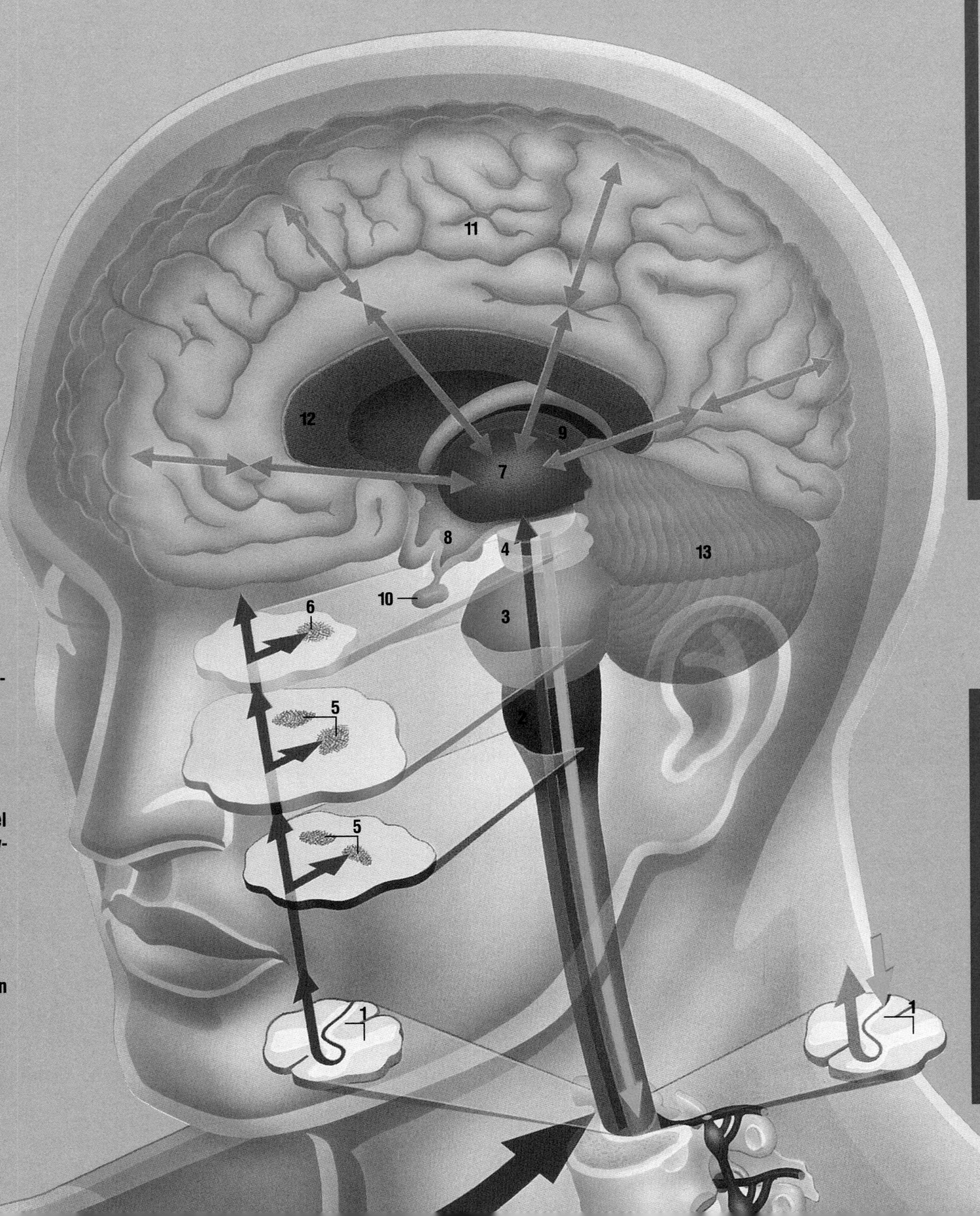

2 FROM SPINE TO BRAIN. Nerve impulses arrive at the dorsal horn (1), an area containing both excitatory and inhibitory neurons. There they cross from one side of the body to the other and are sent up the spinal cord and brainstem to the limbic system and sensory portions of the cerebral cortex. Faster impulses travel directly to the thalamus (7). Slower signals arrive at the thalamus only after detours: Some branch off in the medulla (2) and pons (3) to a dense core of neurons called the reticular formation (5); some are diverted in the midbrain (4) to a part of the reticular formation called the periaqueductal gray (6), which can route signals to the thalamus and also initiate descending inhibitory impulses.

3 ANALYSIS. Signals travel from the thalamus to the hypothalamus (8), hippocampus (9), pituitary gland (10), and other limbic structures, as well as to areas of the cerebral cortex, including limbic, sensory, and motor centers. As the signals reach these areas, the experience described as pain occurs. The sensory and motor areas locate the origin of the stimuli and assign such qualities as sharp or dull, while the emotional centers recognize the unpleasant nature of the sensations. As the incoming messages are interpreted, thoughts and emotional reactions can amplify the sensation or send pain-control impulses back down toward the brainstem.

4 PAIN DAMPENING. Messages from the cortex and the limbic system stimulate the periaqueductal gray in the midbrain to send further nerve impulses down to the spinal cord. These signals trigger the release of painkilling opioids and other chemicals in the dorsal horn, which partially blocks upward passage of impulses arriving from the nociceptors in the injured tissue. Fewer of these entering messages will reach the brain, diminishing the individual's sensation of pain.

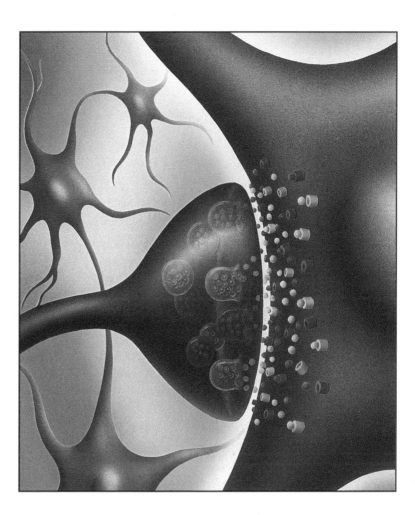

1 A DAMAGE ALERT. An injury activates specialized sensory receptors called nociceptors in the body tissue, sending electrochemical impulses *(red)* to the central nervous system. Two major types of nerve fibers link these nociceptors to the spinal cord: One kind, with a comparatively large diameter and a fatty insulating sheath called myelin, carries impulses swiftly; the other kind, thinner and unmyelinated, transmits signals more slowly.

The Roots of Supersensitivity

An injured person often experiences severe pain when the damaged tissue is later exposed to seemingly benign stimuli. For example, the touch of clothing or even movement of air over the skin can be excruciating to a burn victim—a phenomenon called allodynia. Tissue injury or inflammation causes changes not only in peripheral nerves, but also in spinal cord neurons, amplifying the central nervous system's pain response. Impulses from the peripheral nervous system's nociceptors are typically transmitted when excitatory amino acids *(red)* cross the gap from nerve axon terminals to receptors on the surface of dorsal horn neurons. Researchers think that when nociceptors are persistently stimulated, more neurotransmitters, including substance P *(yellow)*, flow across synapses to activate specialized receptors. This increases the receptive capacity of many dorsal horn neurons, lowering their threshold of excitability and heightening the response to any future input from the site of the injury.

had to stay there and was given nothing but two drinks of lukewarm water and, toward the end, a small chunk of meat to eat. Then he had to endure a further five months of periodic fasting and sexual abstinence before attaining the rank of shaman.

Throughout the late 19th and early 20th centuries, various travelers and anthropologists gathered and published detailed firsthand accounts of shamanic beliefs and deeds. Although these intermediaries often dismissed shamans as charlatans or magicians, many Western thinkers could not help but be intrigued by the tales, especially those having to do with power over extreme pain. How could shamans be stoic in circumstances that would reduce most people to quivering terror or screaming agony? Were they equipped—by some genetic or evolutionary quirk—with a greater capacity for calm or a higher pain threshold than normal? Or, if they felt pain as acutely as everyone else, did they possess uncommon will power? Or maybe their heroic feats were, after all, apocryphal, without basis in reality.

Scientists who long doubted claims of shamanic prowess could hardly be labeled cynics. They were simply operating out of the conservatism that must guide researchers who are almost wholly ignorant of a subject. The ways in which the body conveyed or inhibited pain were only dimly understood even as late as World War II, although anatomists had been reconnoitering the nervous system since the late 19th century. According to the broad outlines they had sketched, scientists thought that the response to pain had evolved to help the human organism avoid harm and, like the stress response, was basically a reflex driven by the nerves.

By the 1950s, however, researchers had begun more detailed mapping to trace how pain signals travel from the source of stimulation through so-called afferent nerves to the spinal cord and then on to the brain (*pages 49-51*). Researchers assumed that the signals sent by the afferent nerves would be conveyed to the brain with an intensity proportional to the stimulus involved. A dull poke in the finger from a blunt stick, for instance, would cause a mild signal to be fired off, whereas a pinprick would trigger a stronger alert, and a cut from a knife an even stronger one. In the brain, the incoming alerts would be processed in a "pain center," a kind of central newsdesk dedicated to sorting out and assessing the importance of these bulletins.

This seemed a perfectly sensible hypothesis, but in the early 1950s,

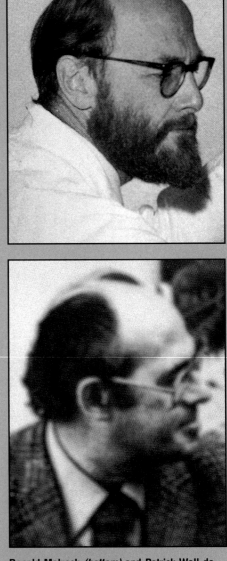

Ronald Melzack *(bottom)* and Patrick Wall devised the gate control theory, describing how pain signals pass through a number of neurological gateways that help govern the brain's response to pain. Melzack and Wall propose that cognitive and emotional forces have far more to do with how people perceive and react to pain than scientists originally thought.

Canadian psychologist Ronald Melzack, then a graduate student at McGill University in Montreal, challenged the assumptions underlying the notion of a pain center. Melzack came to the study of pain obliquely, from his work on canine intelligence and development. During experiments to learn how subjecting young dogs to sensory deprivation affected their behavior later in life, Melzack noticed an odd correlation. Scottish terriers that had been raised in a laboratory kennel, with little stimulation of any kind, seemed, on being let out of their cages, to be impervious to pain. The dogs dashed around the room, and if they accidentally got stepped on or banged their heads, they did not yelp. Intrigued, Melzack tested them further by holding flames to their noses, but even that failed to elicit a response.

Fascinated, Melzack ruled out the possibility that the dogs' systems were failing to generate pain signals and considered it more likely that the signals were somehow being drowned out. Compared with all the other novel information pouring in—the new smells and sights and sounds outside their cages—a mild bump on the head was hardly worth the dogs' notice.

As Melzack later put it, "Since you could have injuries and never feel anything, there was more than a simple connect-the-dot pain pathway to a hypothetical pain center in the brain." During a postdoctoral stint at the University of Oregon in Eugene, Melzack worked to illuminate the terrain between the dots. He and his colleagues discovered that, on reaching the brainstem, pain messages could follow at least five different routes. Significantly, these routes carried the messages not only into the parts of the brain overseeing autonomic bodily functions, but also into the areas governing thought and emotion. To Melzack, the implications were startling and unequivocal. Pain, he realized, is multidimensional, "at once emotional and cognitive and not purely a sensory experience."

Melzack continued his studies in England and Italy and, upon returning to the United States, teamed up with physiologist Patrick Wall to produce a far-reaching new hypothesis of pain. The two researchers called it the gate control theory, and when they presented it publicly in 1965, in the esteemed American journal *Science*, they stirred up—and redirected—an entire field of research.

According to their revolutionary explanation, there are many points, or "gates," at which pain signals traveling toward the brain can be halted by di-

rectives from the brain or the spinal cord itself, or can be modified, to be sent onward with all haste or with lessened urgency. In other words, not all alarm signals generated in the body actually reach the brain, and even those that do may be deemed of minor importance and effectively ignored. Conversely, they may be red-flagged. This was Melzack and Wall's most important conclusion: Since pain messages impinge on parts of the brain that deal with cognition and emotions, it is the interpretation of pain that largely determines the extent to which the pinprick or stubbed toe "hurts." A person's immediate emotional state and overall mental attitude, unavoidably influenced by memories and values, all factor into the pain equation.

Other investigators, galvanized by the boldness of the gate control theory, began devising their own studies to see whether the theory would hold up under scrutiny. For the most part over the last two decades it has. Researchers now regard the human system of perceiving pain as having three principal components: physical, rational, and emotional.

In the physical arena, specialized receptors called nociceptors, found throughout the body's tissues, serve as the first line of response to noxious stimuli. Resembling a kind of three-dimensional mesh, nociceptors interpenetrate the skin with such completeness that an external assault at any given spot will be picked up by several interlacing arrays. When nociceptors fire, their signals race to the spinal cord, where they compete for attention with thousands of other signals streaming in from the body.

Melzack and Wall's "gate," it turns out, is a system that enables one set of signals to override another. If a nociceptor's signal is "loud" enough, indicating severe damage, the central nervous system will send a flash to the muscles, causing them to retract the hand, say, from the handle of a hot skillet. Less-critical alerts from nociceptors may be ignored altogether. A further winnowing of nociceptor bulletins goes on if they are passed on to the brain from the spinal cord. In many parts of the brain, neurons receive the impulses and assess the severity of the external stimulus. Again, an instruction may go out, bidding the body to take some action or to belay movement.

Recent and ongoing research on the physiological threshold of pain suggests that genetic or gender-related hormonal factors might actually cause some people to feel pain less than others. Still, since everyone has basically the same apparatus for sensing pain—the same nociceptors and nerves and neural geography—the wide variation in individual reactions to painful stimuli seems to depend less on any kind of threshold than on the concept of tolerance. It is here that the part of the brain known as the limbic system comes into play, putting its own emotional spin on the body's objective signals of pain.

Given that neurons of the limbic system are involved in generating and regulating emotions, it is not surprising that our perception of hurt depends in part on our attitude toward pain—how much we fear it, or resist it, or indulge it, or suppress it, for instance. In turn, these attitudes rely on such variables as one's family and cultural background, life experience, and psychological makeup.

Tolerance of pain can actually be learned, as, for example, among the Spartans, whose fearlessness in battle and overall imperviousness to hardship were legend in ancient Greece. The young Spartans were rigorously schooled in the austere habits of their elders, taught to be stoic and unyielding, and the modern understanding of pain makes it reasonable to assume that their valor as warriors stemmed from values instilled in childhood.

More substantial evidence of the cultural influence on pain tolerance comes from the intriguing case of the Sherpas of Nepal, long relied on as bearers and guides by those adventurers who challenge the world's highest peaks. Sherpas are renowned for their ability to hike tirelessly at high altitude, lugging 70-pound packs in oxygen-poor air and wearing only thin clothing even in freezing temperatures. A 1982 study comparing the responses to stimuli of a group of Sherpas and Western trekkers revealed clear-cut behavioral differences. The Sherpas accepted pain silently, whereas the Westerners in the group, whose cultures tend to permit or even encourage the public display of suffering, responded more vocally.

So subjective a thing is pain that the immediate psychological circumstances can transform a minor wound into an excruciating ordeal, or, on the other hand, completely erase the immediate impact of a major physical trauma. This effect was noted as long ago as the days of the Roman Empire: "Young soldiers," wrote the philosopher Seneca, "although only slightly wounded, cry and fear the hand of the surgeons even more than the sword of the enemy." By contrast, Seneca noted, longtime legionaries "even if they are pierced through, patiently and without complaint endure that their body, as if it were someone else's, is cleaned of dirt."

Wartime data gathered some 2,000 years later echoes Seneca's observation. In studying the medication records of 150 World War II Allied soldiers who had been wounded during the landing at Anzio, Italy, a researcher found that only 32 percent had requested morphine postoperatively. Yet, among a comparable group of civilians who had undergone similar surgeries, 83 percent had called for morphine. Clearly the difference was one of outlook: To soldiers who had perhaps exhibited heroism and certainly had won a reprieve from battle, the pain of any injury paled beside the fact that they had escaped death. The civilians, for their part, could cheer themselves with no such mitigating thoughts.

Of course, culture and circumstance cannot completely account for individual reactions to pain and its aftermath. For reasons that science has yet to explain, some people seem unusually gifted with the will to transcend adversity. For example, Joe Montana, considered by many to be the greatest quarterback in the history of American football, ruptured a disk in his lower spine while playing for the San Francisco 49ers in September of 1986 and had to undergo surgery. Prognosticators said his career was over, but 63 days after the operation Montana was back on the field leading his team to victory. More than seven years later he was still a dominant force in the game and had come back from an assortment of painful injuries.

Similarly, talented song-and-dance man Ben Vereen was thought to be washed up when, in 1992, he was hit by a truck near his Malibu, California, home. He suffered head and internal injuries, and one leg was so badly smashed that it appeared doubtful that he would ever walk again without aid. But Vereen went at his recovery with a vengeance: intensive physical therapy, from 9:00 A.M. to 5:00 P.M. five days a week. "I'd wanted to do seven days," he said at one point, "but I need to give the therapists a break." After less than a year of this regimen, the 46-year-old Vereen was back on Broadway, singing and dancing in *Jelly's Last Jam* before an appreciative audience that included 25 of his doctors and therapists.

Although science may never be able to account fully for the grit and determination that allow certain individuals to triumph over trauma, modern research has made considerable advances in understanding the neurochemistry that affects how pain is perceived. One giant step came in 1973 when graduate student Candace Pert made a discovery that would lead to a veritable explosion in brain research and illuminate the human body's intricate methods of recognizing and dealing with pain.

In a laboratory at the Johns Hopkins Medical School in Baltimore, Maryland, Pert was working with neuroscientist Solomon Snyder investigating the effects of morphine on brain cells. They employed a procedure in which the cells were dosed with morphine that had been chemically bound to a radioactive dye that would reveal where the morphine ended up. To Pert's surprise, the morphine attached itself to neurons drawn from the brainstem, the thalamus, and the hypothalamus. Chemicals in the body commonly dock with cells, aiding in their functions, but why would morphine, a substance derived from poppy flowers, have its own docking site on neurons? Pert and Snyder surmised that the morphine must have some analogue produced by the body itself and owning similar painkilling properties. When researchers in Sweden and New York confirmed Pert's experiments, the hunt for the brain's own opiates was on.

Barefoot, burdened Sherpa women in Nepal *(above)* and equally laden Nagar porters from northwest Pakistan *(right)* have developed the lung capacity and muscles—and stoicism—to master their harsh environment and demanding jobs, easily outhiking their less-encumbered Western employers.

A breakthrough came in 1975, when John Hughes and Hans Kosterlitz, working at Scotland's Aberdeen University, found a chemical in pig brains that fit the bill. It was a chain built of just five amino acids, the building blocks of proteins. When tested, it latched onto the same morphine receptors that Pert and Snyder had discovered, confirming that it possessed a similar structure to the drug. Hughes and Kosterlitz dubbed their little amino acid chain, or peptide, enkephalin, from the Greek for "in the head." The body, it seemed, manufactured its own analgesic (*pages* 58-59).

The scientific community was electrified. Here was an unsuspected method of communication between the brain and the rest of the body, through a tiny chemical with the specific function of relieving pain. The excitement over this finding had even more to do with what it might indicate in larger terms. An article discussing the opiate receptors in *New Scientist*, Britain's widely read weekly magazine, proclaimed, "Probably the most intriguing aspect of all this is the inescapable implication that there exists in the brain an unexpected 'chemical transmitter system'—a system which may have something to do with dampening pain, but almost certainly has more general effects also."

Within a few years, scientists had discovered dozens more chemicals,

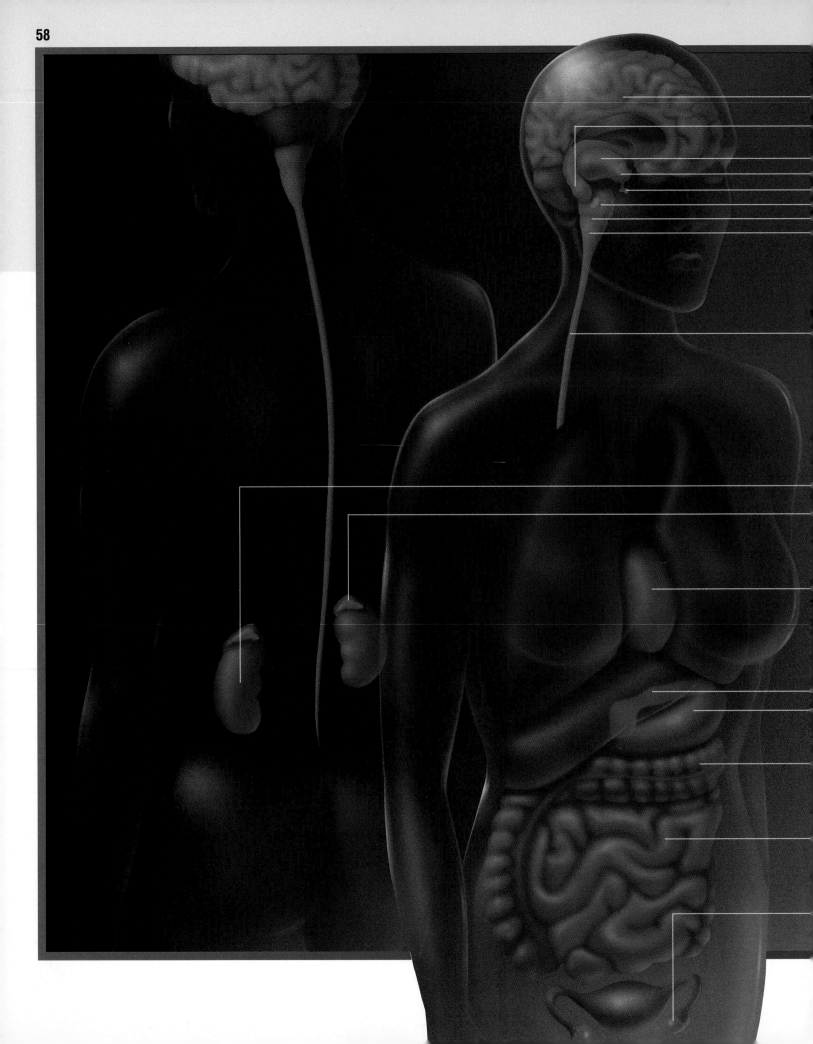

Cerebral Cortex

Hippocampus

Thalamus
Hypothalamus
Pituitary Gland
Pons
Amygdala
Medulla

Spinal Cord

Kidney

Adrenal Medulla

Heart

Pancreas
Stomach

Large Intestine

Small Intestine

Ovary

A Versatile Breed of Biochemical Regulators

Like a glimpse of an unknown continent, the discovery of morphinelike molecules in the brain in the 1970s led to a grand epic of exploration. In the years since those first sightings, scientists have identified a host of kindred chemicals, termed opioids because of their structural resemblance to morphine, a key ingredient of opium. (One of them, enkephalin, is seen in crystalline form at left.) All function as bodily regulators by binding to receptors in the outer membrane of cells. Like their drug namesake, the opioids suppress pain—but that is just one item in their repertoire. They also figure in breathing, body temperature, blood pressure, digestion, sexual activity, fluid balance, response to stress, and even learning and memory.

The distribution of cellular docking sites for opioids reflects this versatility. Receptors are concentrated in the regions of the brain and spinal cord shown in pink on the opposite page. The heart, adrenal medulla, and gastrointestinal organs (*purple*) also have opioid receptors, though not in high concentrations. Receptors may also exist in the pancreas, kidneys, ovaries (*blue*), and testes. Even immune cells can have receptors.

In essence, opioids are small, short-lived proteins with a common active core. They are created in many varieties, with different receptor preferences, different potencies, and other distinguishing traits. Some attach only to receptors close by; others travel long distances through the bloodstream. Yet they seem to function in the same basic way: When they bind to receptors, they inhibit cellular production of other signaling molecules, thus helping to maintain proper levels of activity in the body's ceaseless biochemical interplay.

called neurotransmitters, that are produced by the brain. Moreover, the researchers had discerned the steps in the molecular construction of at least nine neurotransmitters involved in the reception and inhibition of pain. Among them was the original enkephalin, now typically included with the others in a class of chemicals known as endorphins (a contraction of the words *endogenous*, meaning "the body's own," and *morphine*).

More neurotransmitters may yet be implicated as participants in the pain-sensing operation, but the human response to pain is so complex that researchers have their hands full analyzing the peptides they have already identified. For example, every emergency room doctor has seen patients who have broken a finger, wrist, or elbow, driven themselves to the hospital, and failed to register pain until several hours after treatment.

Athletes in the heat of competition are often similarly oblivious to injuries. Long-distance runner Don Paul, for example, once completed the last six miles of a marathon in San Francisco listing to one side, unaware of his posture—or the fact that he had sustained a major stress fracture in his ankle—until after crossing the finish line, in 10th place.

Even more dire injuries have been handled with aplomb. Nineteenth-century Scottish missionary and explorer David Livingstone, for instance, survived a lion attack in Africa and recalled that in the heat of the moment he had felt nothing adverse. "The shock produced a stupor similar to that which seems to be felt by a mouse after the first shake of the cat," Livingstone wrote. "It caused a sort of dreaminess in which there was no sense of pain nor feeling of terror, though quite conscious of all that was happening. It was like what patients partially under the influence of chloroform describe, who see all the operation, but feel not the knife."

Scientists attribute this sort of analgesia under stress to elevated levels of endorphins circulating in the bloodstream. Increased endorphins, then, might have produced the euphoria that overtook fallen climber Rob Schultheis and account as well for the ability of aboriginal peoples to withstand violent rituals.

Endorphins may also be responsible for the so-called runner's high, which kinesiologist Murray Allen of Simon Fraser University in British Columbia has suggested would be better renamed the runner's calm, arguing that this state of overall well-being, which envelops some people after sufficiently strenuous aerobic work-

outs, is less psychedelic than soothing. In fact, circulating endorphins and other opioid peptides are likely responsible for a whole range of states marked by improved mood, including the tranquillity that settles on some women during the last trimester of pregnancy, when endorphin levels are raised. (Conversely, the precipitous falloff of endorphins after delivery— a tenfold drop from peak levels— seems to be the culprit in some postpartum depressions.)

Despite all that remains to be elaborated, physiologists and neuroscientists have provided enough detail regarding pain's mechanisms that physicians have been able to make inroads into the treatment, if not the causes, of chronic pain. Unlike acute pain, which serves the specific purpose of warning against immediate damage, chronic pain can persist, often inexplicably, long after a disease has run its course or an injury has healed. Those suffering from chronic pain may find themselves shunted from one perplexed doctor to the next, all of whose arsenals of diagnostic machinery can spy no organic reason for the complaint.

However, those whose pain falls into this category—hundreds of millions of them around the world, 40 to 80 million in the United States alone—are not necessarily doomed to misery.

They can turn for help to thousands of pain-management centers that have sprung up since the 1950s, when physician John Bonica, anesthesiologist and founder of the International Association for the Study of Pain, pioneered the first such practice in Seattle, Washington. Many major institutions, including the Johns Hopkins Hospital in Baltimore, Maryland, and the Mayo Clinic in Rochester, Min-

nesota, as well as hospitals and clinics abroad, now have comprehensive programs in pain management, designed to help stricken people function as normally as possible.

Advances in pain management have rendered surgery, once advised in some cases, less common. Even the surgical procedures that remain in use have substantial drawbacks. Cordotomy, for example, in which sections of the spinal cord are cut in order to thwart persistent low-back pain, may result in incontinence, impotence, and paralysis. Furthermore, follow-up

On a bus taking them home from Camp Janus in Texas, exuberant 15-year-old Mandi Binkley *(right)* entertains two of her young friends with a song. Mandi, scarred in a gas explosion, is one of many children who attend the camp for young burn survivors—a haven for physical and emotional healing where children learn patience, trust, and improved self-esteem, often from one another.

studies have shown that these drastic measures frequently yield no benefits. As many as 90 percent of patients surveyed after such surgeries have reported only partial relief.

As a result, most chronic-pain specialists favor using a multipronged approach that attempts to deal with not only the physiological but also the psychological factors that may exacerbate chronic pain. To that end, patients work with teams of physicians, psychologists, and physical therapists and participate fully in their own treatment. Generally, the aim is to wean patients from painkilling drugs and to help them devise strategies for minimizing the debilitating effects of their maladies.

When researchers first associated endorphins with the suppression of pain, a few bold surgeons and desperate patients engaged in an experimental surgery to implant platinum electrodes deep in the brainstem along a major opioid pathway. One such case involved U.S. Navy veteran Dennis Hough, who worked on a psychiatric ward and had sustained ruptured disks and a broken back when he was attacked by a patient. Hough remembers the surgery itself, which entailed drilling holes in his skull, as "the most barbaric thing I've ever experienced, including my tour of duty in Vietnam." But, equipped with a transmitter that beamed radio waves to the electrodes, he was able to stimulate the release of endorphins to ease the shooting pains that had become his daily burden.

In more recent years, physicians and others have realized that similar results can be attained without resorting to such drastic methods. The primary neurotransmitters thought to be involved in dampening pain seem to be released under an array of different circumstances. Thus, pain specialists have begun to employ a host of techniques—some of them ancient, some relatively new.

Perhaps the easiest of the practices is relaxation. In 1975 cardiologist Herbert Benson of Harvard developed a technique founded on what he called the relaxation response. His method was based on clinical observations he had made of practitioners of transcendental meditation, who during meditative states were able to decrease their uptake of oxygen, lower their blood pressure, and slow their heart rate—bodily functions that are supposed to be beyond voluntary control. Benson was convinced that he had stumbled on a real, verifiable phenomenon, a "physiological change," as he put it, "that occurs when we alter the state of our consciousness through nondrug means."

Benson devised a kind of one-two-three technique, easy to learn and apply, that he said would prompt the same sort of physiological change as practicing yoga. To achieve the relaxation response, it is necessary to engage for 10 to 20 minutes every day in some repetitive activity that focuses the mind. For example, the iteration of a single word (Benson suggests the word "one") could become the focus, while the practitioner remains passive to any stray thoughts entering the mind. Gradually, the heart rate slows, breaths come less frequently, blood pressure drifts downward, and metabolism slows.

When the brains of those practicing the relaxation response are connected by external electrodes to an electroencephalograph, the machine records an increased output of low-frequency theta waves. This conforms to what is known about electrical impulses in the brain, whose frequencies vary in tandem with the level of conscious awareness. The neurons of a high school student waiting to begin an important exam fire anywhere from 13 to 25 times per second, yielding waves characteristic of states of hyperconcentration. A father reclining on a blanket in a state of calm alertness watching his children play in a public park generates alpha brain waves, with a slightly lower frequency of

Pain Control from Within

Each year, millions of people experience debilitating pain that resists standard medical treatment. Some patients find temporary relief in the form of drugs, nerve blocks, electrical implants, acupuncture, massage, osteopathy, and chiropractic spinal manipulation. With improved insight into the workings of pain, specialists are increasingly turning to methods that enable patients to manage pain by tapping their inner resources.

An underpinning of these innovative methods is a recognition that chronic pain often results from a combination of physical vulnerability, "learned" responses, and neurochemical changes. Consciously or subconsciously, the individual may perceive some sort of reward in continued distress—staying home from work, for example, or kind treatment from others. Coping behavior that de-

velops in response to injury, such as favoring a limb, rubbing the injured area, or wincing, may bring only short-term relief and can, in fact, perpetuate the pain. In addition, stress, fatigue, negative thoughts, anxiety, depression, and anger can all trigger changes in the central nervous system that exacerbate pain, decreasing levels of opioids—the body's natural painkillers—and elevating levels of substances such as cortisol and catecholamines, which may amplify pain.

To some degree, however, pain can also be unlearned. Adjustments in belief, thought, and activity can condition the mind and body over time to let go of unnecessary pain. The approaches explained on the following pages are among those being used successfully to help individuals take command from within.

eight to 13 cycles per second. The neurons of a person practicing the relaxation response or a yoga trance fire off only four to eight times per second, yielding theta waves. And a person in a deep sleep customarily displays brain waves that cycle one to three times per second, the so-called delta waves.

The relaxation-response approach is akin to biofeedback, a method for controlling normally involuntary physiological processes that was once dismissed as quackery. Biofeedback is now widely accepted as a legitimate therapy technique, with demonstrated success in the treatment of chronic pain (*page* 67). The fundamental notion behind biofeedback is that by receiving information about our own brain wave activity we can, through mental effort, retard the rate at which our neurons fire, thereby slipping into a waking state resembling the most restful phase of slumber. Biofeedback seems especially good for relieving muscle-related pain such as tension headaches and a disorder known as temporomandibular joint syndrome, which can cause jaw pain and dental problems from incessant teeth grinding during sleep.

Acupuncture, also an efficient method for limiting pain, originated in ancient China. In its earliest incarnation, acupuncture was part herbal magic, part primitive medicine. Starting

sometime before 2500 BC, Chinese healers began practicing something known as moxibustion: They burned the flowering plant artemisia, of the genus that includes sagebrush and wormwood, and set cone-shaped embers of the plant at key points on the body. In this way they believed they stimulated the circulation of *qi* (pronounced "chee"), a vital life force thought by them to course through the body and the universe alike.

Acupuncture evolved around the same time. This method of therapy envisioned the body as laced with a network of qi-carrying tracts, called meridians, which could be stimulated by stone needles. Historically, acupuncturists have identified as many as 365 points on the body, called acupoints, each of which is supposed to relieve pain in a specific organ or limb, or to stimulate healing by promoting the flow of qi. Modern acupuncturists employ only about 100 points and have substituted surgical steel needles for stone ones.

During the 1970s, a series of papers by Dr. Bruce Pomeranz of the University of Toronto described possible mechanisms to explain acupuncture's effectiveness. Chiefly, the practice seems to fight pain with pain, using a

form of mild irritation to minimize more severe discomfort. When an acupuncturist inserts needles into acupoints, nociceptors in that region fire off signals alerting the central nervous system. The central nervous system, in turn, sends back a signal to the nociceptors to quiet down, while the brain releases endorphins. Placing needles randomly over the body produces mild analgesia in the same fashion, but experiments conducted by Pomeranz and others clearly demonstrate that when needles are placed in traditional acupoints, release of the brain's own painkillers is substantially heightened.

Among the pain-reduction techniques, modern treatment centers often rely on behavior-modification therapies designed to help people put their physical suffering in a different context. To do this, pain specialists must occasionally fill the roles of educator, counselor, and even priest. The first lesson is that chronic pain, whether it is caused by an identifiable disease or by a mental maladaptation, can only be conquered one step at a time, with the full will and devotion of the patient—and often with the involvement of the patient's family members, who may unconsciously behave in ways that encourage the patient to focus unnecessarily on pain.

Usually, after an initial evaluation,

Strategies to Unlearn Pain

Cognitions—what we think and know—can profoundly influence how intensely pain is felt. Confidence in the effectiveness of a therapy, sense of personal control, and the meanings attached to the pain may all influence perception. An approach called cognitive restructuring helps people identify and change ideas and attitudes that amplify their pain.

In essence, cognitive restructuring teaches patients to interrupt self-destructive thoughts, dispute maladaptive beliefs, and replace negative mental images. For example, a patient may believe that her back pain is caused by permanent scar tissue in her spinal column. Visualizing the ineradicable scar tissue only adds to her anxiety. But she can convert this unsolvable mental problem to a solvable one by replacing the image of the scar tissue with one of knotted muscles. With practice, the imaginary muscles can be mentally "unknotted," decreasing her sense that the pain is uncontrollable.

The body, too, can be retrained. It is natural and desirable to restrict physical activity in response to an injury. But when pain persists after tissue has healed, remaining sedentary can exact a penalty: Muscles tighten, joints stiffen, and weakness sets in; as a result, attempts at exercise become increasingly painful, usually resulting in even lower levels of activity.

To break this cycle, therapists use a technique called shaping. The patient establishes a baseline—the length of time an action, such as walking, can be performed before the pain increases. If a man with severe back pain, for example, can tolerate walking for 10 minutes, he is asked to walk regularly for a shorter period—perhaps five minutes—several times a day. He plans the activity by time rather than tolerance and stays on schedule, even if he feels slightly worse or better on a particular day. Gradually, he begins to dissociate walking from the feeling of pain. Over a period of a few weeks, he increases his walking time to the baseline level of 10 minutes, and then beyond. Both body and brain are reprogrammed, and pain is progressively reduced.

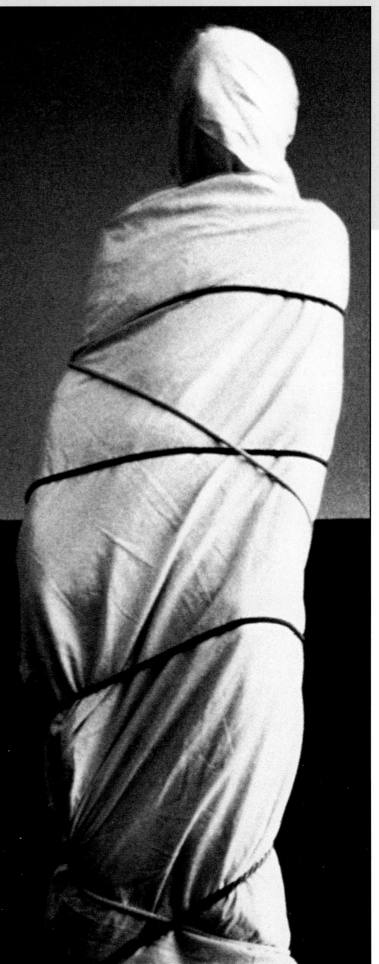

behavior-modification patients enter group counseling, where they explore their fears—"Are my headaches being caused by a brain tumor that somehow doesn't show up on the CT scan?" "What will happen to my family if I die from breast cancer?"—and learn how their own feelings of guilt, inadequacy, failure, and self-pity act to make the pain worse. Cognitive therapy teaches them to replace negative thoughts ("I can't handle this") with positive ones.

British specialists A. W. Diamond and S. W. Coniam encourage patients at their clinic in Bristol to confront pain consciously, in part by talking to themselves whenever they hurt. Diamond and Coniam suggest that patients tell themselves something like, "All right, I'm feeling tense. That lets me know that I should take slow deep breaths and relax, so that I can change to another strategy. I will not let the pain overwhelm me. I will let my thoughts handle the situation just one stage at a time. I will do something positive to confront these sensations."

In other words, for some people positive thinking apparently works, just as the late Norman Vincent Peale claimed that it did. Peale, who died in December 1993, was the minister whose religion-laced exhortations sold to millions of readers under titles such as *The Power of Positive Thinking*, *Stay Alive All Your Life*, and *You Can If You Think You Can*. Peale inspired a whole generation of post-World War II Americans, and science now seems to be confirming that he hit upon a genuine phenomenon. Peale claimed that through a combination of persistence, self-confidence, and faith in God, people could accomplish the virtually impossible.

A collector of stories, Peale regaled lecture audiences and readers with inspiring tales of triumph. He told about Irwin Rosenberg, a junior naval officer who overcame four bouts with cancer, won a special act of Congress forcing the navy to reinstate him after he had been discharged because of his illness, and went on to become rear admiral of the Seventh Fleet. Peale also recounted the story of Ben Franklin of Topeka, Kansas, who learned to walk again after breaking his back in four places in a climbing accident. The upbeat minister claimed that all people who overcome obstacles share in common a refusal to surrender hope, and he advised those who aspired to the same invincibility to "Never, never settle for defeat," and "Drop the word 'impossible' from your mental processes."

Although researchers have yet to pin down precisely how positive thinking works its magic, they suspect it must activate mechanisms in the body in some fashion similar to the placebo effect. Placebos are therapeutic techniques or medications such as sugar pills or injections of distilled water that improve a patient's condition despite having no true medicinal properties. Placebos have long fascinated physicians because they can actually lessen symptoms. (Inert chemicals that cause symptoms to worsen, because a person expects them to do so, are termed nocebos.)

Placebos' efficacy against pain appears to be related to the release of endorphins, but beyond this, researchers cannot explain how they operate. What is clear is that a patient's attitude and expectations concerning his or her condition, along with the degree of comfort the patient feels with doctors and other caregivers, all have an effect on recovery, and the more positive the patient's overall state of mind, the better.

Physicians have really just begun to explore what Norman Cousins, former *Saturday Review* editor, called "the biology of hope." Cousins, grappling with a degenerative and sometimes fatal back disorder called ankylosing spondylitis, was all but dismissed by the medical community when, in the mid-1970s, he first started inspiring audiences with the story of his remarkable return to health as a consequence of a hearty indulgence in laughter. But by

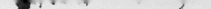

The Elixir of Relaxation

Relaxation is an indispensable component of a good pain-management program, contributing to relief by reducing muscle tension, quieting nervous arousal, and promoting the release of opioids that dampen pain sensations (*pages* 58-59). The goal of pain-related relaxation techniques is a state of calm achieved by concentrating attention on one thing to the exclusion of all others. Many methods are used—self-hypnosis, progressively tensing and releasing muscle groups, imagining warmth or some other soothing sensation, repeating a word or phrase, and focusing on an object or on a mental image. With all of these techniques, mental discipline is essential.

One approach, biofeedback, gives the mind an external assist. A patient learns to curb nervous arousal by watching or listening to instruments that monitor such telltale cues as breathing, muscle tension, perspiration, body temperature, or blood pressure. For example, a woman might visualize picking up a handful of warm sand on a sunny beach—an image that relaxes her and produces a drop in blood pressure as resistance in her blood vessels is lowered. Bringing such autonomic functions to her conscious attention gradually affords a measure of control over them. In time, she learns how different levels of tension feel and conditions herself to relax without the monitoring equipment. Newer biofeedback devices can be used while a patient is engaged in activity, not just sitting quietly. This allows easier transfer of the relaxed state to daily life, away from a clinical setting.

1979, the medical community had come around. Cousins, no longer a gadfly but a kind of expert, received an appointment as adjunct professor at the University of California at Los Angeles School of Medicine and continued to spread the word that positive emotions play a significant role in the healing process.

Neither Cousins nor any other advocate of positive thinking seriously advised that conventional medical know-how be abandoned, only that it be supplemented by proven psychological strategies. David Spiegal, a physician at Stanford University who has helped cancer patients deal with pain through hypnosis, envisions an expansion in the definition of healthcare beyond mere physical intervention. "We have to add to the surgical and medical interventions," Spiegal has said, "a standard component of treatment that involves helping the person who has the disease deal with it and feel supported through it."

Of course, the physical travail of injury or disease is not the only kind of pain—or perhaps even the worst kind. Those who have survived terrible ordeals that involved psychological anguish unfailingly attest to the worth of never losing hope and of searching out mental images that provide solace and inspiration. Survivors of concentration camps, prisoners of

Music, Laughter, and Relief

Age-old strategies of emotional uplift can provide valuable help in pain reduction. Music, for example, has been shown to counter tension and anxiety—an effect accompanied by changes in heart rate, blood pressure, breathing rhythm, hormone levels, and many other physiological measures. Studies suggest that patients undergoing cataract operations feel less anxious and need less sedation if they listen to music through headphones during the surgery.

Similarly, research has demonstrated that some women in labor perceive the experience as less painful and stressful when certain types of music are part of the process; 71 percent of mothers who delivered their babies with music playing in the background told researchers during one survey that they had felt "relaxed." The same story is seen in cancer therapy. In one

study, cancer patients participated in twice-daily 45-minute listening sessions. Some were treated to relaxing music, while others heard only a tone. After three days, the two groups switched. A significant number of subjects reported that the music brought greater pain relief than did the tone.

Laughter, too, possesses pain-relieving powers. A heartfelt laugh stimulates the body, briefly raising the heart rate, ventilating the lungs, and exercising muscles. Laboratory studies have shown that it also increases brain alertness, boosts immune activity, and—most striking of all—improves the blood's ratio of painkilling opioids to stress hormones such as catecholamines and cortisol. Some of the beneficial effects, including the relative reduction of stress hormones, last as long as 24 hours after a mirthful episode.

war, and kidnap victims have all reported that they fortified themselves largely through mental effort.

Viktor Frankl detailed many of the mental tactics that he employed during his three years of imprisonment in a German work camp during World War II. In his 1963 book, *Man's Search for Meaning*, Frankl tells of finding "refuge from the emptiness, desolation, and spiritual poverty" of the concentration camp by thinking of his wife, who had been separated from him and sent to another camp. Although he had no idea whether she was alive—she did not, in fact, survive—Frankl communed with her in spirit, enduring the bone-chilling cold, whippings, forced marches, and exhausting ditchdigging by taking strength from the image he held in his mind. Sometimes, Frankl wrote, he sensed his wife's presence so vividly that he felt he could reach out and touch her.

One time Frankl was digging trenches in the frozen ground of Bavaria. "The dawn was gray around us; gray was the sky above; gray the snow in the pale light of dawn; gray the rags in which my fellow prisoners were clad, and gray their faces," Frankl wrote. "I was again conversing silently with my wife, or perhaps I was trying to find the reason for my sufferings, my slow dying. In a last violent protest against the hopelessness of imminent death, I sensed my spirit piercing through the

Painting Themselves a Brighter World

Fear and anxiety show on the faces of two young Jewish inmates (*above*) of the infamous World War II Theresienstadt concentration camp in German-occupied Czechoslovakia. With public relations in mind, the Nazis billed Theresienstadt as a model town, a gift to the Jews from Adolf Hitler. In fact, the camp was a hellish dumping-ground used to intern high-profile Jews such as government officials, academics, musicians, and artists. The victims' families went with them.

Prisoners soon found that Theresienstadt was hardly the paradise that the Nazis had promised. In this death-filled ghetto, inmates lived in cold, cramped, vermin-ridden buildings, trying to fight off disease and stay alive on rations far too meager to fuel their long hours of forced manual labor. Theirs was a misery compounded by fear; most knew that Theresienstadt was often merely a turnstile to the death camps of Germany and Poland.

One of the ghastliest aspects of Theresienstadt was that children were not exempt from its horrors. Often they had to endure not only the camp's inhumane conditions, but separation from their parents as well. However, the adult inmates, believing that the children were perhaps the only hope for the future, lavished on them all the care they could. The adults taught academic lessons in secret and encouraged the children to express themselves with poems, stories, and drawings. The surviving artwork includes the idyllic *Garden* on the right, by 12-year-old Ruth Cechova. The picture expresses the resilience and optimism that the human spirit can sometimes show, even in the most appalling conditions. Tragically, the optimism was ill justified. Of the 15,000 children of Theresienstadt, perhaps no more than 100 survived.

enveloping gloom. I felt it transcend that hopeless, meaningless world, and from somewhere I heard a victorious 'Yes' in answer to my question of an ultimate purpose."

Soldiers who have been wounded and captured in battle often must withstand physical and psychological pain for long periods of time. Many of those who make it home testify to the beneficial effects of overcoming their fears and maintaining the certitude that they will be rescued or released.

During the 1991 Persian Gulf War, U.S. Army flight surgeon Major Rhonda Cornum underwent her baptism by fire. When her helicopter was downed by Iraqi antiaircraft guns, the 36-year-old major sustained two broken arms and took a bullet to the shoulder. Captured by Iraqi troops, Cornum was sexually assaulted while she was being trucked to her prison, and she spent days without medical attention. She was held captive until the war ended eight days later.

To cope, Cornum devised a series of strategies to keep her sanity. Along with singing and praying, she mentally put her family members in what she called the "home drawer" and closed it so she would not worry about them. She also imagined herself as a "hu-man radio antenna" that could project positive feelings to her husband, Kory, an army surgeon on duty in Saudi Arabia. Cornum worked to keep her mind off of her own suffering by concentrating on bolstering the spirits of two other Americans who were imprisoned with her. In an autobiographical account, *She Went to War*, Cornum recalled that although she knew that being a prisoner would be hard, "it was better than being dead."

Researchers will probably require many more decades to gain a fuller comprehension of how such evanescent things as thoughts can affect the body. But what they have learned so far about survival and the brain promises to help focus the inquiry.

For example, endocrinologist and author Deepak Chopra believes that neurotransmitters may hold the key to people's ability to prevail in the face of seemingly unbearable circumstances. "Neurotransmitters," Chopra wrote in his 1989 best-selling book *Quantum Healing*, "touch the life of every cell. Wherever a thought wants to go, these chemicals must go too, and without them, no thoughts can exist. To think is to practice brain chemistry, promoting a cascade of responses throughout the body."

To think positive thoughts is, therefore, to stimulate the systems that prime the body for action and dampen pain. "Mind by any definition is nonmaterial," Chopra goes on, "yet it has devised a way to work in partnership with these complicated communicator molecules."

Neurotransmitters may indeed be the medium of communication between mind and body, but, as Chopra notes, these chemicals are not the motive force. Intangibles such as altruism, love, will power, concentration, and faith are among the nonmaterial agents of the mind that seem essential to survival. Even supposing that such mental qualities entail neurochemical interactions, it is possible that precise explanations of how they enhance human endurance may elude the scientific grasp.

Like the farthest reaches of the subatomic realm, which actually alter on being observed by the instruments of physics, the human capacity to conquer seemingly unbeatable odds must perhaps remain fundamentally mysterious. Still, researchers and individuals have found ways to tap the untold reserves of the human body, whether to fight disease, overcome physical injury and pain, or remain mentally stable in the face of cruel circumstances. Such tools may also open the door to peak performances and flights of creativity.

A jubilant Terry Anderson waves to friends and reporters in New York City upon his return after seven years as a hostage in Beirut, Lebanon. With him is his six-year-old daughter, Sulome, who was not yet born when he was captured. Shackled in tiny cells with other hostages, the former journalist persistently prayed, made up games, conjugated French verbs, and kept a secret diary to preserve his sanity.

CHOOSING TO SURVIVE

The everyday business of living in a modern society does little to prepare anyone for a protracted ordeal. Yet when ordinary people are thrust into extreme hardship by an accident or other twist of fate, they often prove more resilient than they ever imagined possible—more resilient, in some cases, than their physical resources would seem to allow. The reason, survival experts agree, is that physique is only part of the story. Along with threats to the body—deprivation, exposure to the elements, injury, and so on—survival situations frequently involve hazards of an emotional kind: loneliness, uncertainty, self-pity, and fear. An ability to counter such emotional dangers may spell the difference between life and death.

The mind can address the challenges of survival situations in a number of ways, analyzing the threats and opportunities, organizing a plan of action, even bringing humor to bear on the problems. But one mental asset lies at the heart of almost every account of survival: will power, the determination to endure. Those who make it through terrible ordeals usually recall moments when a choice was required—to go on or give up. Of all the tests of strength that arise along the way, this is the most likely to determine who lives and who dies.

OVERCOMING THE FIRST SHOCK

A shipwreck or a plane crash can transform comfort and security into utter chaos in a matter of seconds. Not all survival ordeals begin so suddenly, but most eventually produce the sense of a once-orderly world spinning out of control. The attendant emotional shock can leave victims prey to a potentially deadly threat—fear of the unknown.

This fear is a heightened version of the kind of apprehension triggered by more ordinary encounters with the unknown, such as a new job or school. It is a normal response to a life-threatening situation, but it must be kept under control lest it grow into panic and lead to paralysis or some irrational action that could compound the dangers. According to survival experts, transcending fright is the first order of business in staying alive when the world seems to have come undone.

Proper training can greatly reduce the time required to overcome fear, a point that is emphasized in survival-training programs such as those run by the U.S. Army for Special Forces candidates. The best recovery method is to take small steps to make the immediate circumstances less inimical and debilitating. Tending to injuries, seeking or creating shelter, finding food and water—all these tasks help not only to increase physical comfort but also to reestablish a sense of control.

Once the primary needs are met, fear is further checked by assessing the facts of the situation. Survivors begin to beat back the unknown by investigating their surroundings and taking an inventory of the tools and supplies available that can help to keep them alive. As fear recedes, planning can begin, setting the stage for actions that can lead to a return to safety or to rescue by others.

CALMLY SOLVING PROBLEMS

After the first moments of fear have passed, the long haul of survival begins, perhaps to the accompaniment of hunger, thirst, pain, and adverse weather. In the hours, days, or even weeks that follow, a crucial survival tool will be a reasoning mind, one that is able to view the ordeal not as an overwhelming set of threats but as a puzzle to be solved.

Lauren Elder, a young woman who was stranded on a snow-covered mountain in California by a plane crash that killed her companions, tapped her problem-solving abilities when she stood at the brink of a sheer granite cliff. To reach safety—still many miles beyond—Elder knew she would have to descend the rockface, but at first she saw no route down. She nonetheless decided she would find a way, and after long scrutiny, Elder began to discern crevices big enough for fingers and toes. When she had mapped a path, she edged over the precipice—and soon found herself almost flowing down the granite face. "Everything was so finely balanced," she later recalled, "that I knew I could do no wrong."

Like many survivors, Elder had tested a barrier with her powers of observation and reason, probing it patiently until the answer emerged. The key to such success, survival experts emphasize, is a positive attitude, a sense that the puzzle will have a solution. But humor, too, can be of help. Many survivors remember moments when their predicament seemed almost ridiculous, like something out of fiction. Such an ironic view gave them the sort of perspective they needed in order to look at their problem in an analytic way, assessing the situation calmly and discovering that the odds of survival were not as long as they first appeared to be.

A BATTLE FOUGHT BY STAGES

Mountaineer Joe Simpson had already survived two falls on the face of a 21,000-foot peak in the Peruvian Andes. The first had broken his leg, and the second had separated him from his climbing partner, who thought him dead. Now, a day later, Simpson was crawling snail-like across a glacier toward his still-distant base camp. Exhaustion, dehydration, and the searing pain of the badly injured leg left him dazed and drowsy, but a voice within drove him on.

The climber's immediate goal was much closer than the camp where he could find help. He had picked out a particular feature among the waves of snow ahead, then looked at his watch and set a half-hour deadline for reaching it. An inner voice would startle him out of occasional pauses of daydreaming and tell him he must reach the chosen spot in time. Once there, he would repeat the exercise. Simpson called the technique that

brought him safely down Siula Grande a "mind game." Survival experts see it differently: Setting goals and sticking to them is essential to success in a hostile environment. Incremental goals like Simpson's hummocks of snow are important because they present manageable challenges and offer small successes that help keep spirits up.

Simpson's refusal to be deterred by pain is a staple of survival instruction. Military survival schools emphasize this point, teaching soldiers simply to accept pain as a fact that has little bearing on their actual ability to do things. Pain is sometimes described as proof that the body is working as it should, reporting injuries and ailments. But fear of pain or discomfort must never be allowed to stand in the way of the ultimate goal—staying alive. One Special Forces officer is fond of quoting the German philosopher Nietzsche: "What does not kill me makes me stronger."

BUILDING A TEAM TO FIGHT FOR LIFE

A leaky raft, overloaded with six men and two women, was all that remained of the *Pride of Baltimore* in July of 1986. Knocked down by a sudden squall, the schooner went under in little more than a minute, throwing her crew into the sea 240 miles north of Puerto Rico. Four people drowned. The rest huddled on the raft, wet, scared, and lost in their own thoughts as darkness fell.

Sunrise brought them together, and as they salvaged floating pieces of gear and organized their slender rations, they became a crew again. Solidarity served them well as passing days took their toll. Tears of frustration brought consolation from others; a hallucinating crew member who got up to take a walk was restrained by his fellows. When another lost a precious piece of his daily half-biscuit ration, the rest broke off bits of theirs to replace it. "I have seven friends who saved my life," one survivor said after the four-day ordeal, "and we'll always be tied together."

The crew of the *Pride* demonstrated the kind of teamwork that can improve the odds of survival for every member of the group. Sometimes this cohesion arises naturally. In other instances it stems from strong leaders who take charge. Group dynamics are not necessarily smooth in survival situations, however; not everyone finds it easy to subordinate personal preferences to the greater good. But even strong leaders must weigh the opinions of all rather than demand blind obedience. Disagreements, while they may be momentarily disruptive, can often improve an idea and, no less important, can lead to a consensus that strengthens the group's commitment to mutual support.

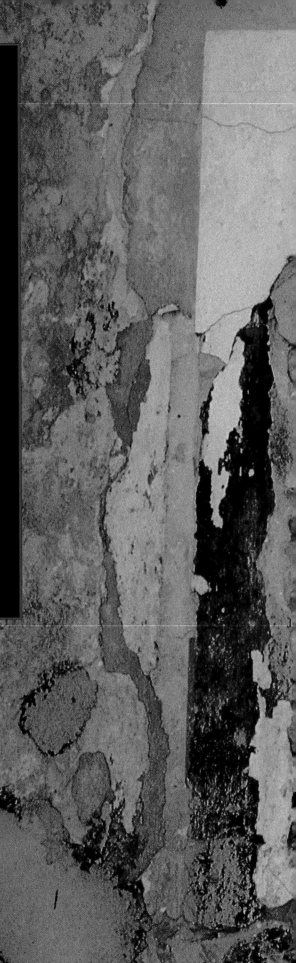

LOOKING BEYOND THE MOMENT

After weeks of darkness and isolation in a cramped Hanoi prison cell, U.S. Navy pilot James Stockdale discovered a window on another, brighter world: his past. Bit by bit the captive pilot, whose plane had been shot down over North Vietnam in 1965, re-created long-lost situations in minute detail—childhood birthday parties, for example, or favorite schoolrooms. "You can draw the past out of your head with remarkable recall by easing slowly toward the event you seek and not crowding the mind too closely," he later said. Treasures gleaned from such forays helped sustain Stockdale through eight bleak years of captivity. He emerged with his spirits undimmed and went on to become an admiral.

The past is just one of the refuges available to the mind. People forced into long-term solitude have occupied themselves with such mental activities as assembling a car from its thousands of pieces; setting up a cinema and recalling the dialogue of a film running there; or planning a walking trip across Europe, with daily activities worked out in complete detail.

Even the present affords mental sanctuaries. Despite all difficulties, there is usually some time to rest and focus on visual pleasures lying beyond the hardships and dangers of the moment. Clouds, light, trees, birds, ocean waves—all have their own intrinsic beauty, independent of the grim facts of the situation. Many survivors have expressed that such shifts in perspective can be restorative, lifting fear and anxiety and lending the mind the serenity it needs to think and plan effectively.

THE SURVIVOR'S HEIGHTENED VISION

Looking back on their ordeals, most survivors see little that would tempt them to court danger again, although they often discern lessons that they can apply in their daily lives. Some, however, remember the experience as an adventure, a time of heightened sensibilities difficult to re-create in ordinary settings, and they may even act on those memories. For these individuals, facing danger and hardship is so stimulating that they willingly return to it again and again.

Their outlook is rooted in the pleasure of exercising human abilities and instincts that were honed by millennia of evolution in the wilderness but are largely dormant in modern societies. These enthusiasts learn to focus their attention as hunter-gatherers did, developing a sharpened awareness of the world that seems at times to in-clude a sixth sense. "I can feel things that can't be seen," says one survival-trained veteran of the U.S. Army Special Forces. "I've opened my mind, body, and soul to the environment around me, to the point where I am one with my environment."

Even survivors who have no wish to ever repeat their experiences some-times speak of them almost with reverence. One man who endured a harrowing march across Europe to a German prison camp during World War II wrote of living "in such a state of absorption that I was hardly aware of the sufferings we endured. Neither the hunger, thirst, nor fatigue that we fell heir to during our long trek, under a scorching sun, touched anything basic in me. I realized that this was a unique experience and it engrossed me completely."

3

Power to Perform

For Olympic shooter Bob Foth, stillness is everything. One of his specialties is the Three-Position Rifle event, in which he takes prone, kneeling, and standing positions while firing a .22-caliber rifle at a bull's-eye target 50 meters away; the center of the target, where top competitors put most of their shots, measures 10.4 millimeters in diameter, smaller than a dime. At the instant the trigger is pulled, Foth tries to be as still as a statue to avoid displacement of his aim. He is very good at achieving this state of near-perfect motionlessness— one of the stellar performers in his sport, in fact. At the Olympic Summer Games held in Barcelona in 1992, he took the silver medal in the Three-Position event, missing the gold by .8 out of a total possible score of 1,309. On other occasions and in other tests of marksmanship, this former mathematics teacher has set more than 100 U.S. records and seven world records.

At the U.S. Olympic Training Center in Colorado Springs, Foth sometimes checks on his technique with the aid of a laser sighting device attached below the barrel of his rifle. As he aims, the laser produces an infrared dot on the target. Although the dot is invisible to the unaided eye, Foth and his coaches can view it on a black-and-white television monitor, revealing even the most minuscule movements of the rifle during sighting. The mere beating of Foth's heart causes the telltale spot of light to dance about on the target 50 meters away, leaping as much as an inch off line with each pulse.

At Foth's competitive level, regularly missing the target's center by an inch would bring certain defeat. To help dampen the effects of the heartbeat (as well as vibrations caused by, of all things, digestion), shooters usually wear one or two sweatshirts covered by a stiff outer jacket made of canvas or leather. Physical fitness is also an important factor: Foth lowers his heart rate by riding a bike. But, as with other top shooters, Foth's chief means of countering the pulse problem is to fire between heartbeats.

Such precision requires the shooter's total concentration—a kind of complete immersion in the visual situation, including the infinitesimal wanderings of the rifle's sights at the critical moment. In a competition, Foth begins with a series of rhythmic breaths that are coordinated to specific tasks in his preshot routine. "During each of those inhale-and-exhale cycles, I know what I should be thinking about and what I should be visualizing, what parts of my body I should be focusing on relaxation in, where the rifle should be pointed, and what I should be doing with my visual focus." He breathes in and lifts the stock of

the rifle; he breathes in again, and now he's pointing the .22 at the target; he breathes again, and he's sighting directly on the bull's-eye. Then, utterly still, aware of only the sights and the center of the target, he prepares to pull the trigger. If his heartbeat were amplified, the soundtrack of the moment would go like this:

Ka-thump . . . ka-thump . . . BLAM! . . . ka-thump . . . ka-thump.

To an observer, shooting may look effortless. Yet it is exhausting. "After a match," Foth says, "about all I can do is put the rifle down. I've used so much mental energy that I'm pretty much a basket case."

Rick McKinney is a world-class performer in the related sport of archery, and he too hones his technique at the Olympic Training Center in Colorado. Instead of a .22 rifle, he uses a 47-pound bow to fire a carbon-graphite arrow at a target 98.6 yards away. On the Colorado practice range, he has worked with two scientists to iron out problems of mind and body. One is biomechanist Charles Dillman, former director of the training center's Sport Science and Technology Division. When McKinney was preparing for the 1984 Olympics, Dillman analyzed the archer's performance with the aid of

16-millimeter movie cameras and special platforms that measure the shifting distribution of weight under each foot. "One of Rick's problems," Dillman noted later, "was that his horizontal stability was weak and that he needed more strength in his arms to serve as a perfectly still platform from which to release the arrow. We learned that a one-millimeter tremor in his arms would produce a nine-centimeter error 90 meters downrange." When McKinney corrected these deficiencies, his average score rose by more than five percent, a major gain for a competitor already among the best in his sport.

At the Olympic Training Center, McKinney has also consulted Daniel Landers, a pioneer in the applications of biofeedback in sports. Biofeedback involves the monitoring of a covert physiological process, such as heartbeat or skin temperature, so that it becomes overt—usually visible or audible. When the brain is made aware of the process, it can sometimes gain a measure of control over it.

In McKinney's case, the problem was not a technical flaw in performance but rather the aftermath of shooting. The archer had begun developing headaches after competitions because he was tightly squinting his nonsighting eye for several seconds during each shot. During practice sessions, Landers placed elec-

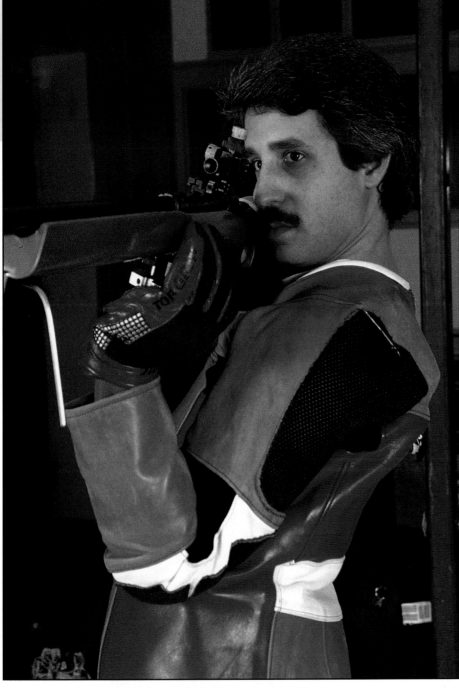

Adopting a balanced stance that helps him maintain statuelike steadiness when he is firing at a target 50 meters away, U.S. Olympic shooter Bob Foth checks the sights on his .22-caliber rifle before a practice session. He wears a heavy leather jacket and gloves to minimize the transmission of his heartbeat or other involuntary bodily movements to the gun.

trodes next to McKinney's nonsighting eye and hooked up an apparatus that turned the electrical signals into a sound similar to the white noise of television static, enabling McKinney to hear his muscle tension. With the help of this biofeedback device, McKinney was able to reduce what was a three- to five-second squint per shot to a single blink of the eye. The headaches disappeared.

In their different ways, shooter Bob Foth and archer Rick McKinney exemplify a revolution in progress: The world of sports, specifically designed to test and showcase human physical ability, has gone high-tech. Today, many of the finest athletes work closely with physiologists, nutritionists, biomechanists, and other specialists to sharpen their performances to the maximum and then maintain the edge. Computers, high-speed cameras, and special sensors are used to reveal, analyze, and refine even the smallest details of technique. Training programs are developed to ensure optimal musculature, stamina, and other physical characteristics.

The physical component of training is only half the story, however: The sports revolution also extends to the mind. At one time, the psychology of athletic competition was a fairly simple business. Coaches spoke of the importance of such mental attributes as "desire" or "grit" in eking out the

final, winning increment of performance, and they motivated their athletes with versions of the philosophy famously articulated by football coach Vince Lombardi to the Green Bay Packers in training camp: "I want total dedication from every man in this room, dedication to himself, to the team, and to winning. Winning is a habit, gentlemen. Winning isn't everything, it's the only thing."

Today, the stoking of competitive fires is just one component of the mental aspect of sports. Many top athletes now work with sport psychologists to improve their performance. These specialists may stress the usefulness of preparing for competition with mental imagery—thought pictures that help put the athlete in the right frame of mind or that can actually serve as a kind of practice. Sport psychologists teach methods for countering negative thinking and promoting relaxation and concentration. And to better understand the ingredients of peak performance, they are exploring the phenomenon known as flow—a state of pleasurable mastery that represents a sports optimum.

The role of the mind is now seen as critical in the upper reaches of sports, whether in track or table tennis, weightlifting or wrestling. Shane Murphy, sport psychologist with the U.S. Olympic Committee, observes: "When you have two athletes with similar talent

and training, the outcome of the competition between them will ultimately come down to what's between their ears." Bob Foth speaks for many athletes when he states, "In Olympic shooting, the difference between winning and losing is 100 percent mental." The same, of course, is true of many other sorts of human endeavor. Referring to the psychological tools developed for athletes, Brad Hatfield, professor of kinesiology at the University of Maryland, says, "The implications go way beyond sports. Whether it's an airline pilot, musician, surgeon, or CEO, everyone's goal is achieving a peak performance."

In sports, at least, peak performance is an ever moving target. The record books tell a tale of virtually

nonstop improvement in recent decades. Consider swimming: In the 1972 Olympic Games in Munich, United States competitor Mark Spitz set seven world records on the way to winning an equal number of gold medals, and, over the course of his whole career, he established 26 world records in the freestyle, butterfly, relay, and medley events. Today, those once-awesome marks have all been surpassed, some by large margins.

Similar wholesale topping of records has occurred in many other sports. In 1972 alone, for instance, the 5.49-meter world record for the pole vault, set two years earlier by Christos Papanikolaou, was broken four times, ultimately by Bob Seagren, who cleared the bar at 5.63 meters. By 1992, pole vaulter Sergei Bubka had pushed the world record to 6.13 meters. And when speed skater Bonnie Blair won the 500-meter event with a time of 39.10

Two balance beam performances sum up 20th-century progress in gymnastics: At far left, Danish women gymnasts give a decorous but undemanding "exhibition" at the 1908 Olympics in London; at near left, superbly trained American gymnast Betty Okino executes a planche, or handstand, during the 1990 Goodwill Games in Seattle, Washington. Female gymnasts did not compete in the Olympics until 1928—and not in individual events until 1932.

seconds in 1988, she not only set a new world record for women, she shaved nearly a tenth of a second off the winning time for men in the 1976 Olympics. More of the same seems likely as the secrets of body and mind continue to yield to science.

In 1922 British researcher Archibald V. Hill received a Nobel Prize for his studies of human muscle, remarking later, "If physiology can aid in the development of athletics as a science and an art, I think it will deserve well of mankind." During the years that followed, science began to make its first halting advances into the world of coaching, providing some hard physiological facts on stamina and other matters. In 1927, for example, Law-rence J. Henderson, a professor at the Harvard Medical School, launched a landmark investigation into the nature of fatigue by putting subjects through rigorous tests to discover the effects of wind, cold, changes in nutrition, and differences in altitude. Few coaches showed a craving for the sort of scientific data he supplied, however; they were more comfortable assessing physical potential by guess-work and trial-and-error methods.

Beginning in the late 1920s, physiologist Wallace O. Fenn of the University of Rochester and his colleague Rodolfo Margaria anticipated the marriage of science and sport by studying such things as the elasticity and internal friction of human muscle. Continuing their research over the years, the scientists went on to examine how oxygen debt, lactic acid, and gravity affect muscular strength.

After World War II, scientists in the Soviet Union seized the research baton, exploring human potential from a number of angles—initially unrelated to sports. Among other investigations, they studied the mental and physical characteristics of Holocaust survivors, hoping to identify traits that lie behind exceptional feats of endurance. In the 1950s, Soviet space scientists explored the possibility of teaching cosmonauts to control such supposedly involuntary bodily functions as heart rate, temperature, and muscle tension as well as emotional reactions to stressful situations such as zero gravity. The inspiration for these studies was the ancient yogic arts of India and Tibet. The term *yoga*—Sanskrit for "yoking"—refers to a complex religious training system meant to achieve unity between all the parts of the body and the mind, and ultimately to unify the individual with God.

Some of these insights were put to work in the sport programs of the Soviet Union and other Communist-bloc countries. From the earliest days of Communism, Party leaders had favored recreation and physical training for the masses, as a way of helping workers to remain healthy and productive. For decades, the leaders disdained the Olympic Games as a "bourgeois" activity, but after World War II—seeing that Olympic victories would have considerable propaganda value around the world—they decided to participate. Government officials were told to "raise the level of skill, so that Soviet sportsmen might win world supremacy in the major sports in the immediate future."

The officials responded by creating networks of state-supported sport schools: 40 such elite institutions were established in the USSR; other bloc countries followed suit, with East Germany alone setting up 25 sport schools. No effort was spared in developing future stars. Scouts tested three- and four-year-olds for athletic promise, and the chosen few were taken from their parents and inducted into the sport programs. Because the schools had lavish state support, these would-be Olympians enjoyed some exceptional comforts—the

reason most parents agreed to the arrangement. But their lives were highly regimented. Six-year-old skaters trained three or four hours every day and devoted additional hours to doing push-ups, running, practicing ballet, and watching training films. They rarely saw their parents, rarely enjoyed an outing such as a trip to the zoo, and always had to put their sports ahead of their studies.

Political indoctrination was a prominent ingredient of the children's educational fare. As one East German manual for training young divers put it, "The success of socialist countries in sport has had a remarkable impact in the anti-imperialistic battle for peace and détente. Our opponents understand this and are doing everything in their power to stop or, at the very least, to limit our success. Consequently, it is our duty to use the merits of our socialist social structure to go well prepared into this class war and to be victorious."

The results of this enforced dedication were nothing short of extraordinary. For example, in the Summer Olympics between 1964 and 1976, the Soviet Union won 156 gold medals and East Germany 79; the United States, by comparison, won 148. Even

small Communist-bloc nations such as Rumania and Bulgaria fared brilliantly for their size.

Although much of the Communist bloc's success at the Olympics can be attributed to the unprecedented scope and almost life-devouring intensity of the sport programs (and also to the extensive use of steroids), one factor behind their victories deserved the admiring attention of the entire sports world. The architects of the Soviet-bloc sport programs demonstrated, beyond any doubt, the value of a truly scientific, mind-plus-body approach to performance.

Charles Garfield, a former world-class weightlifter who has a doctorate in clinical psychology and who has written extensively on peak performance, had the lesson brought home to him in a delightfully bizarre encounter with Soviet sport psychologists in Milan in 1979. After a formal function at the villa of the mayor of Milan, Garfield and the Soviets began walking the streets of the quiet Italian city after midnight in an unlikely search for an open gym in which the Soviets could demonstrate some of their mental-training theories. Unsuccessful in their quest, the group returned to the mayor's house and awakened him. The mayor, no doubt impressed with the diplomatic urgency of the situation, made some calls and located a gym with weights.

Well after 2:00 A.M., Garfield found himself hooked up to an alphabetical array of EEG, ECG, and EMG machines designed to measure brain, heart, and muscular activity. As Garfield recalled it, the Soviets—"looking grave and deliberate"—interviewed him about his conditioning and weightlifting background. He told them that, at one point, he had been able to bench-press 365 pounds, but that it had been eight years since he had seriously trained. Next, they asked him to lift the absolute maximum he thought he was now capable of. Garfield man-aged to press 300 pounds—but "with enormous difficulty," as he put it.

At that point, the Soviet researchers went to work evaluating Garfield's height, weight, body fat, metabolic rate, and blood. Satisfied with their readings and computations, they asked him to lie on his back, and they proceeded to guide him into a state free of any tension. "I was fully awake and alert," he remembered later, "yet every muscle in my body relaxed, and I felt more at ease than ever before in my life." Garfield imagined his arms becoming heavy and warm. After some 40 minutes, the Soviet sport

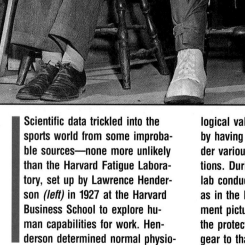

Scientific data trickled into the sports world from some improbable sources—none more unlikely than the Harvard Fatigue Laboratory, set up by Lawrence Henderson (left) in 1927 at the Harvard Business School to explore human capabilities for work. Henderson determined normal physiological values for young adults by having volunteers exercise under various environmental conditions. During World War II, the lab conducted military research, as in the low-temperature experiment pictured above, comparing the protection of cold-weather gear to that of ordinary clothing.

psychologists asked him to sit up slowly and stare at a bench press holding 365 pounds of weights. He was instructed to imagine the sound of the weights clanking against each other as he grabbed the bar, to feel his breathing patterns, to hear his grunting as he thrust the weight off his chest. They talked him through the process over and over again. Then, astonishingly, Garfield bench-pressed the full 365 pounds.

Inevitably, the systematic use of the imagination that was pioneered in the Eastern-bloc schools became a fixture of top-level sport programs around the world. Two related techniques—both used in Garfield's postmidnight introduction to Soviet methods—are staples of this aspect of training: mental imagery and mental rehearsal.

At its most basic, mental imagery is the visualization of an object, scene, or sensation as though it were actually happening or present in reality. The harried executive who is able to relax by merely imagining what it will feel like to sit on the porch of a weekend cottage has employed mental imagery to reduce stress. Athletes may use images that represent what they want to achieve or that induce a particular state of mind prior to competition—a desired level of relaxation, concentration, or perhaps energy.

Sometimes athletes imagine complex sequences of images. As an ex-ample, Richard Suinn, a psychologist who has worked extensively with U.S. Olympic athletes, cites the procedure used by one veteran pentathlete to clear his mind between events: He would imagine drawing a large circle and putting the number 10 inside it; next, he would mentally draw a small-er circle inside the first one, move the 10 into it, and give the number 9 to the outer circle; he would then draw an even smaller circle inside the first two, move the 10 into it, move the 9 into the previous circle, and put the number 8 in the first circle. The se-quence, which could continue indefi-nitely, had the effect of eliminating the tension of the previous event and focusing him on neutral activity while waiting for the next one.

Mental rehearsal—also called men-tal practice—is essentially imagery in motion. Rather than imagining a still picture or a precise pose, such as the executive's weekend cottage or the pentathlete's numbered circles, men-tal rehearsal requires that the athlete "see" a scene in motion as it would actually happen, including sounds, smells, and tactile sensations. When accompanied by relaxation exercises, says Richard Suinn, mental practice "apparently is more than sheer imagi-nation. It is a well-controlled copy of experience, a sort of body-thinking similar to the powerful illusion of cer-tain dreams at night. Perhaps the ma-jor difference between such dreams and [mental rehearsal] is that the im-agery rehearsal is subject to con-scious control."

Some researchers believe that, dur-ing mental rehearsal, the brain actual-ly sends nerve impulses out to the appropriate muscles; these research-ers argue that a well-conditioned ath-lete who properly imagines a task is training muscles almost as well as if the task were being physically per-formed. This contention, known as the psychoneuromuscular theory, does not appear to be supported by the weight of scientific evidence, however. In one study indicating that mental re-hearsal does not work the same way as the real thing, neurologist Peter Fox of the University of Texas Health Sci-ence Center in San Antonio monitored the brain activity of a group of sub-jects in two stages—first as they were imagining various body motions, then during the actual performance of the motions. He found that the same brain areas were activated in both cases—except for the motor cortex, the portion of the brain that sends direct orders to the muscles. Psychol-ogist Shane Murphy sums up the situ-ation this way: "All the current evi-dence points to the conclusion that

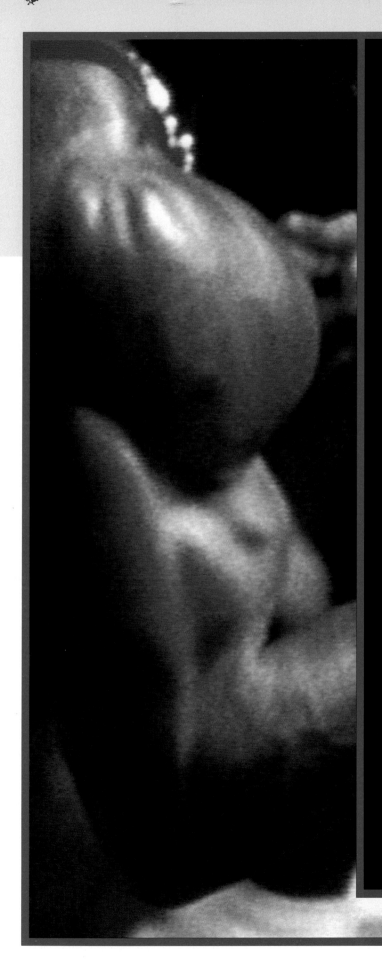

Dangerous Sources of Unnatural Power

In a world where athletes continue to accomplish the impossible, some participants feel compelled to boost their natural abilities with drugs and other illegal "performance enhancers." This disturbing trend is not limited to competitors at the professional or Olympic level. Many teenagers, hoping to achieve strength and muscle definition, are also turning to drugs, and in ever higher dosages. But in their quest, they are taking enormous risks that can have dire consequences.

Certain drugs or techniques are associated with particular activities. Anabolic steroids and other synthetic hormones, for example, are popular ways for athletes in strength-oriented sports to short-cut nature's more arduous path to muscularity. The chemicals generally do promote muscle bulk and strength, but only when combined with strenuous exercise and when taken in extremely large doses, which can have serious effects on the mind as well as the body.

For archers and shooters, who strive not for bulk but for a steady aim, beta blockers are the enhancers of choice. These drugs lower the heart rate and blood pressure, but they can also cause heart problems and, in men, can lead to impotence. Some endurance athletes, such as bicyclists, get extra stamina from a powerful natural source—their own blood, removed, stored, and reintroduced just before a race, a practice known as blood doping. And a few competitors still rely on stimulants ranging from caffeine to amphetamines. These drugs can delay fatigue and help athletes "psych up" for an event, but with prolonged use they can lead to heart failure. The following pages describe the physical processes at work in two of these performance-enhancing techniques.

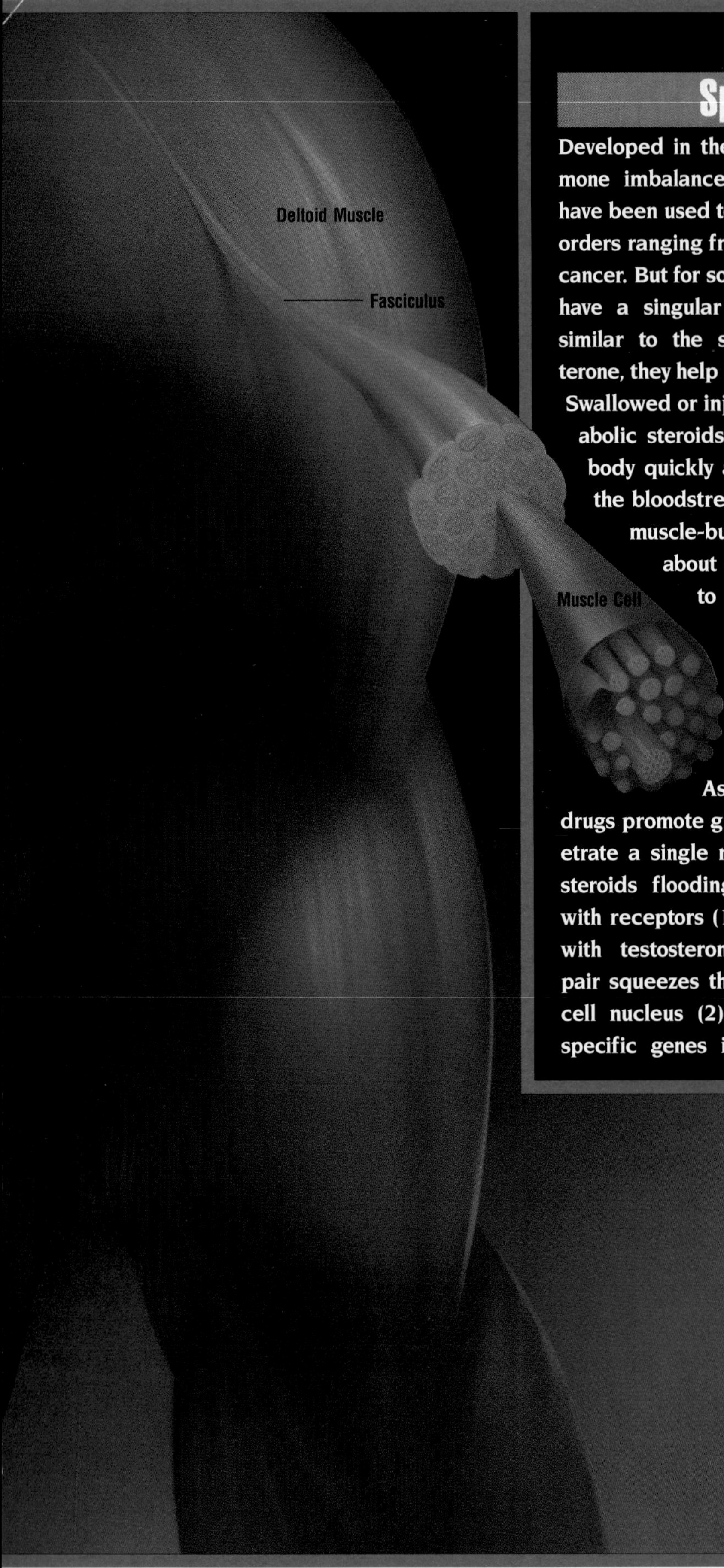

Deltoid Muscle

——— Fasciculus

Muscle Cell

Spurring Growth in a Muscle Cell

Developed in the 1930s to treat hormone imbalances, anabolic steroids have been used to battle a host of disorders ranging from anemia to breast cancer. But for some athletes, steroids have a singular appeal: Chemically similar to the sex hormone testosterone, they help build bigger muscles. Swallowed or injected, almost all anabolic steroids introduced into the body quickly attach to proteins in the bloodstream and thus have no muscle-building effect. Only about one percent manage to seep through capillary walls into muscle tissue—hence the large doses needed to produce measurable results.

As illustrated here, the drugs promote growth once they penetrate a single muscle cell. At right, steroids flooding the cell hook up with receptors (1) that naturally bind with testosterone. The interlocked pair squeezes through a pore in the cell nucleus (2) and interacts with specific genes in the DNA (3), the body's coded blueprint. Key portions of the DNA code are copied onto a strand of messenger RNA (4), which travels into the cytoplasm (5) and instructs a ribosome to start creating chains of amino acids (6), the basic ingredients of protein. Throughout the cell, these chains permeate fibrous shafts called myofibrils (7), adding bulk to the muscle proteins myosin (*thick filament*) and actin. As these filaments enlarge, so does the muscle.

This growth comes at great expense, however. Steroid users sometimes fly into so-called 'roid rages—surges of violent behavior possibly sparked when the drugs attach to testosterone receptors in the brain. The chemicals also can produce unwanted androgenic effects. For instance, women may notice chest and facial hair, a permanent deepening of the voice, breast shrinkage, and infrequent menstruation. In men, the drugs can cause sterility and prompt the development of femalelike breasts. Other side effects for both sexes may include acne, permanent liver damage, and heart problems.

MUSCLE FIBER. Close scrutiny of tissue from the shoulder's deltoid muscle *(left)* reveals a complex arrangement of fibers within fibers. Each individual strand, known as a fasciculus, is actually a bundle of threadlike muscle cells, some reaching 20 centimeters in length. Within a cell, such as the one magnified at right, a nucleus rests alongside yet another set of fibers called myofibrils, which house the vital protein filaments myosin and actin.

Muscle Cell

Steroid

Receptor

1

2

Nucleus

3

5

Messenger RNA

4

Amino Acid Chain

6

Ribosome

Myofibril

Myosin

Protein

Actin

7

Artery

Red Blood Cell — Oxygen

1

2

3

Bulking Up on Blood

The muscles of endurance athletes need a steady flow of oxygen from the lungs to keep up the pace. In the body, this shuttle service is provided by red blood cells (1). Since more oxygen means greater stamina, some athletes try to boost their supply of red blood cells through blood doping.

Weeks before an event, some of the athlete's blood is removed (2) and stored. The body, sensing the deficit (3), generates more red cells. Just before competition, when the cell count is back to normal (4), the stored blood is reinjected (5), adding more oxygen-bearing cells (6). Blood doping defies detection, but its consequences can be severe: An excess of red blood cells can clog capillaries, possibly causing a heart attack or stroke.

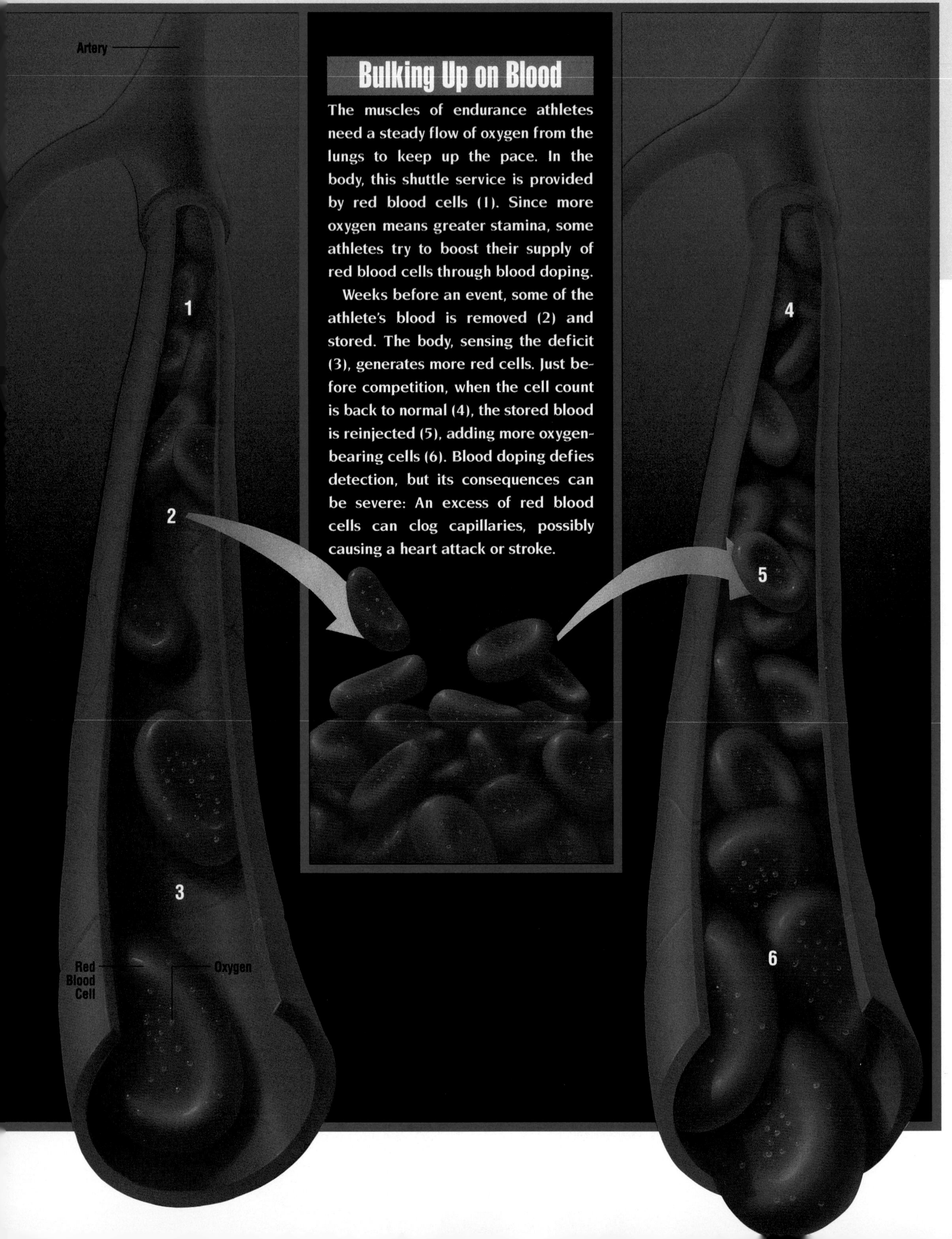

4

5

6

visualization works because it replicates the brain activity that controls human movement, so that an athlete gives his brain a good workout by using mental rehearsal."

Even if only the brain is getting practice, numerous studies indicate that mental rehearsal works. In one classic study done in 1978, a graduate student named Barbara Kolonay tested basketball players at New York's Hunter College. Her research focused on free throw shooting and involved a large number of subjects and proper use of control groups. Some of the players began the testing process with relaxation exercises. Then, while sitting in straight-backed chairs, they repeatedly imagined the process of shooting free throws—being handed the ball by the official, hearing the crowd, eyeing the rim, releasing the ball, and making the shot. The players using mental rehearsal improved their accuracy as much as 15 percent over their previous accuracy rate.

For mental rehearsal, an important requirement, along with relaxation, is that the athlete imagine a flowing movement, not just a series of still mental pictures. Basketball Hall of Famer Bill Russell could do this in almost symphonic variety. Describing

how he prepared for games, he wrote: "I was sitting there with my eyes closed, watching plays in my head. It was effortless; the movies I saw in my head seemed to have their own projector, and whenever I closed my eyes, it would run. With only a little mental discipline, I could keep myself focused on plays I had actually seen, and so many of them were new that I never felt bored." Greg Louganis, gold medalist in the platform and springboard diving events at the 1984 and 1988 Olympics, was another master of mental rehearsal. He always pictured his dives from the point of view of an observer, watching his imagined self perform; he also listened to music while making these imaginary dives, thus linking his timing to auditory patterns as well as visual ones.

In sports, mental rehearsal has innumerable applications, but it is especially effective for improving proficiency in repetitive motions that are roughly similar each time—a golf swing or a pole vault, for example, rather than never-quite-the-same actions such as a kickoff return in football. Psychologist Daniel Druckman, who directed a lengthy study of mental imagery for the U.S. Army, says the technique works best on "anything that has a clear pattern of steps—you do this before you do that."

In recommending mental rehearsal as a training tool, researchers do not

suggest that it can ever take the place of, say, tackling drills or wind sprints for beginning football players. They see it as useful primarily for well-conditioned athletes whose skills are already in place. Their point is that a gymnast who has dismounted from the rings a thousand times can maintain his competitive edge with the help of relaxation and mental rehearsal rather than relying solely on physical repetition of the movement. And they concede that, apart from its value as a way of keeping the brain in practice, mental rehearsal may involve a degree of placebo effect—a self-fulfilling expectation. As the mental-imagery researchers Linda Warner and M. Evelyn McNeill have written: "Motivation, expectancy, and a willingness to step beyond our limited concepts about what is possible all play a role in what we are able to achieve." In short, these things tend to work if we really want them to.

While imagery techniques hone athletic performance with no tool other than the brain, biofeedback gives the mind technical assistance. In its essence, biofeedback is a communications strategy with an educational payoff: When monitoring instruments reveal hidden aspects of what the body is doing, the brain can sometimes learn how to control those otherwise clandestine processes.

Biofeedback earned its spurs in the realm of medicine. It has long been used in the treatment of so-called functional disorders, including migraine headaches, rectal incontinence, hypertension, bronchial asthma, and many gastrointestinal disturbances.

The sports world employs biofeedback in a number of ways, some of them essentially medical, such as in the rehabilitation of injuries. Yet another use for the technique is in helping to create and maintain correct athletic postures and movements. And biofeedback may also help with subtle but significant performance flaws. For example, Arizona State University's Daniel Landers, a leading researcher in the field, used biofeedback to help a female collegiate archer who was in a severe slump, shooting well below her scoring average of previous years.

When the archer's respiration was monitored, it became apparent that she was taking a very slight inhalation at the instant she released the arrow. Landers set up an apparatus that made the archer's breathing audible during practice sessions. With this biofeedback she was able to modify her breathing pattern—and as a result, her scores rose dramatically.

In his biofeedback studies, Landers has tuned in on brain functioning through electroencephalography. His EEG readings have shown that, just before elite archers release an arrow, a burst of low-frequency alpha waves, indicative of a relaxed state, occurs in the left side of the brain. Recently, he monitored the brain wave patterns of some novices as they took a 15-week training program in archery at Arizona State: As they gained skill, the familiar alpha pattern emerged. Brad Hatfield of the University of Maryland has found the same pattern in shooters: Just before they pull the trigger, neurons in the left cerebral hemisphere fire in an alpha pattern.

For decades, neuroscientists have been aware that the left and right sides of the brain divide up mental labor to some extent. Generally speaking, language and sequential processing of information are specialties of the left hemisphere; spatial relations and pattern recognition ("simultaneous processing of information," as Landers puts it) are specialties of the right cerebral hemisphere. Although the issue of left- and right-brain functioning is complex and fraught with controversy, it may well bear on how peak performance is achieved in sports—and in many other activities, for that matter.

The findings of Landers and Hatfield suggest that, as the shooter or archer prepares to fire, left-brain sequential analysis is being suspended—relaxed, in effect—and control is shifting to the right brain. With that shift, according to Landers, "They're not focusing on every bit and piece of the skill itself or going over the steps in their mind. They're just doing it more holistically." He has even built an experimental biofeedback training program around the left-right distinction. He attached archers to a monitoring device that revealed the degree of alpha wave relaxation in both sides of the brain. Gradually, the archers gained some control over the phenomenon, but their command of the different hemispheres varied. Archers who developed the greatest ability to relax the left side of the brain performed significantly better than those who tended to relax the right hemisphere.

Many sport psychologists draw a connection between the relaxed, trancelike state associated with alpha waves and a state known as flow—a term introduced in 1974 by psychologist Mihaly Csikszentmihalyi (pro-

A Chair That Helps Bring Out the Best

"A biofeedback training module" is how the designers of the Alpha Chamber System (*below*) describe their creation, used as a training tool in sports, medicine, and other fields. While unmistakably a product of the space age, the apparatus also has an elemental aspect: It looks like nothing so much as an egg. The heart of the system is a cushioned chair whose curved shell shuts out auditory and visual distractions, promotes a feeling of security, and helps users to slip into a state of relaxation within a few minutes. This serene condition, characterized by mental receptivity, is merely the beginning. It sets the stage for practicing various stress-reduction techniques—deep breathing or progressive muscle relaxation, for instance—that can later serve in competition. To help users gauge their inner state and thus gain greater control of it, the system monitors and displays changes in muscle tension, brain wave activity, breathing, and heart rate.

In addition to biofeedback equipment, the Alpha Chamber includes a sophisticated audiovisual system to help athletes learn mental rehearsal of skills. On a large video screen, a sprinter, for example, may watch a tape of himself executing a perfect start. At the same time, speakers built into the chair will supply appropriate sounds: a starting gun, a cheering crowd. Such vivid imagery will help impress the moment of personal mastery on the athlete's mind—the better to replicate it in reality.

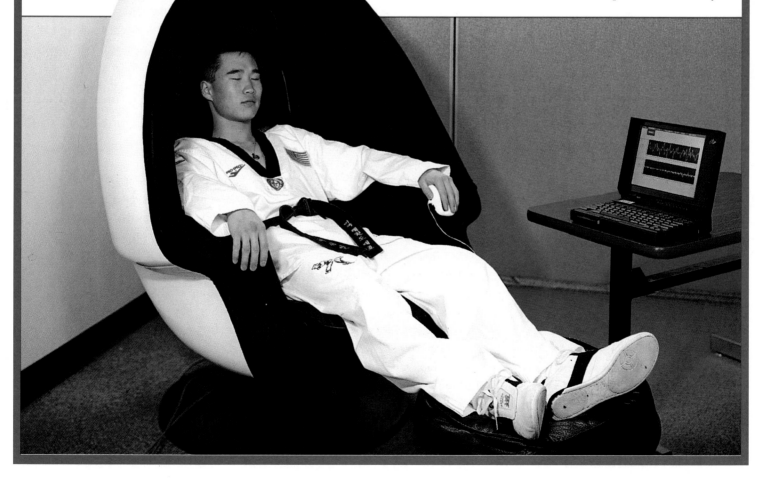

With his 16-pound shot at the ready, a shot-putter fixes his attention on the task just ahead—unleashing all of his strength in a perfectly timed sequence of movements. Many of today's athletes have been able to improve their performance dramatically by using techniques designed to train the mind as well as the body.

nounced "chik-semi-high") of the University of Chicago. In the context of sports, Csikszentmihalyi defines flow as the inherently enjoyable feelings that occur when there is a near-perfect match-up between an athlete's capabilities and the demands of the situation. "When the information that keeps coming into awareness is congruent with goals, psychic energy flows effortlessly," he writes. "There is no need to worry, no reason to question one's adequacy. But whenever one does stop to think about oneself, the evidence is encouraging: 'You are doing all right.' The positive feedback strengthens the self, and more attention is freed to deal with the outer and inner environment." He calls flow "the psychology of optimal experience." It has also been termed "the optimal energy zone." Csikszentmihalyi and other researchers have found flow to be closely associated with peak performance.

One vivid account of a flow experience that resulted in peak performance comes from the British track immortal Roger Bannister. The year was 1954—before sport psychology had even emerged as an applied discipline. Many runners of the day assumed that a four-minute mile was physically impossible; some experts even offered medical "evidence" in support of this view. Bannister, however, believed not only that it was

within human capability but that—as competition sharpened and training methods improved—even faster times were inevitable.

Bannister chose to make the attempt on the track at Oxford, where he had run his first race, and he enlisted two other runners to set the pace on the first three laps. After one false start, the gun fired again and Chris Brasher took the lead. "I slipped in effortlessly behind him," Bannister wrote later, "feeling tremendously full of running. My legs seemed to meet no resistance at all, as if propelled by some unknown force." At the half-mile mark, the time was one minute 58 seconds. "I was relaxing so much that my mind seemed almost detached from my body," Bannister continued. "At three-quarters of a mile the effort was still barely perceptible; the time was three minutes .7 second, and by now the crowd was roaring. Somehow I had to run the last lap in 59 seconds." Chris Chataway took the lead, but at the beginning of the backstretch, with 300 yards to go, Bannister jumped past him.

"I had a moment of mixed joy and anguish, when my mind took over. It raced well ahead of my body and drew my body compellingly forward,"

Bannister wrote. "There was no pain, only a great unity of movement and aim. The world seemed to stand still, or did not exist. The only reality was the next 200 yards of track under my feet." With the noise of the crowd in his ears, he wrote, "I felt at that moment that it was my chance to do one thing supremely well."

Running on empty, Bannister lunged across the finish line, breaking the four-minute barrier by .6 second—an achievement that ranks among the greatest in the history of track and field. That same year, 52 other milers broke the four-minute mark—clear proof that mental limitations, not physical, kept virtually a whole generation of middle-distance runners from reaching their full potential.

The concept of flow is not entirely new; it actually has ancient religious antecedents. As Mihaly Csikszentmihalyi notes: "The similarities between yoga and flow are extremely strong; in fact it makes sense to think of yoga as very thoroughly planned flow activities. Both try to achieve a joyous, self-forgetful involvement through concentration, which in turn is made possible by a discipline of the body." He also sees the martial arts of the East as a form of flow: "The warrior strives to reach the point where he can act with lightning speed against opponents, without having to think or reason

about the best defensive or offensive move to make. Those who perform it well claim that fighting becomes a joyous artistic performance, during which the everyday experience of duality between mind and body is transformed into a harmonious one-pointedness of mind."

Many modern scholars have sought to understand the nature of such moments. In the 1960s, the psychologist Abraham Maslow investigated so-called peak experiences by interviewing or corresponding with more than 300 people in research for a book titled *Toward a Psychology of Being*. Maslow wanted to know what happened to these individuals—how they perceived things—when they were at the height of creative production, experiencing intellectual insights or enjoying "certain forms of athletic fulfillment." Among his observations was that "one aspect of the peak experience is a complete, though momentary, loss of fear, anxiety, inhibition, defense, and control. . . . The fear of being overwhelmed by the 'instincts,' the fear of death and insanity, the fear of giving in to unbridled pleasure and emotion, all tend to disappear or go into abeyance for the time being."

Few top athletes would describe their exploits that way, yet peak or optimal experiences, in the Maslow or Csikszentmihalyi sense of the terms, are a familiar part of sports. When

Second Wind: Paying Back the Body's Debt

Almost any amateur cyclist, runner, or aerobic-exercise enthusiast has experienced the phenomenon known as second wind. A few minutes into a workout, you are short of breath, your chest hurts, your legs burn. Then suddenly you feel a fresh surge of energy. You can breathe again without pain, your limbs no longer feel like lead, and thoughts have changed from "I don't think I can" to "I know I can."

The explanation may lie in a metabolic shift that occurs during exercise. At the start of intense physical activity, the body gets much of its energy anaerobically, meaning "without oxygen": The energy is extracted from glucose stored in the muscles by a relatively inefficient, oxygen-free chemical process. A by-product of the process is lactic acid, which builds up in the muscles and causes cramping and labored breathing. This condition is referred to as oxygen debt, since oxygen is needed to break down the accumulating lactic acid. To pay off the debt, the body's oxygen-delivery systems must gear up until they match the level of activity. The balancing out is what we feel as a second wind.

Athletes in good shape do not experience second wind. Their lungs and circulatory systems are efficient enough to bring lactic acid and oxygen into balance quickly, averting the unpleasant effects felt by non-Olympians.

basketball players have a magical game in which they are making 70 to 80 percent of their shots—a shooting average that even top professionals cannot maintain for a full season—they almost universally speak of a euphoric sensation in which they genuinely believed they could not miss a shot, an all-consuming confidence that overcame hesitancy and self-doubt. "You were unconscious out there!" a sports announcer might say to the star in a postgame interview, and, in a way, that would be right. For a brief period of time, the athlete probably was unconscious of many of the self-defeating thoughts that seem to fight for control of the emotions.

In a book titled *Inner Skiing*, authors Timothy Gallwey and Bob Kriegel wrote that the fear of letting go—the "fear of flying," as they put it—is one of the most debilitating problems for the novice skier. Having finally conquered it, however, "we become so absorbed in what's happening that we stop thinking, fearing, doubting, self-instructing, or analyzing. This quieting of the mind helps our performance immeasurably because of the resulting increase in awareness." But like the faint star in the galaxy that seems to vanish if stared at directly, a realization of this "exalted state of consciousness" may bring about its end, said Gallwey and Kriegel. Just as one cannot constantly take the pulse of a relationship and hope it will maintain spontaneity, neither can one sustain a peak performance by repeatedly analyzing it in progress.

Much has been written about the concept of "letting go" and how the removal of one's self-critical, inhibiting thoughts is essential to achieving peak performance. Psychologist Charles Garfield has interviewed hundreds of athletes about their finest moments and writes that "letting go" is often mistakenly equated with being "laid back" or indifferent to one's fate. "Nothing could be further from the truth," he says.

A more accurate view, according to Garfield, is that the athlete "learns to trust the complex subconscious mechanisms that ultimately determine peak performance, and out of that trust he or she is able to relinquish the conscious or willful controls that inhibit these subtler processes." When the athlete is unable to conquer these self-defeating thoughts, performance almost always suffers—usually, Garfield contends, in one of four ways. In his words:

1. The athlete tries too hard, performing under the impression that the harder one struggles, the better the outcome.

2. The athlete worries about past mistakes, and the fear of repeating such mistakes inhibits performance. Muscles tighten up and actions become tentative and unsure.

3. The athlete becomes overly concerned about the outcome of a game or a play, causing his or her movements to be cautious, anxious, and mechanical.

4. The athlete is overly aroused and excited and forgets that the performances are spontaneous and natural. Excessive arousal becomes a source of stress, with the athlete feeling that every action is a life-and-death struggle. When the athlete is anxious to do the right thing, conscious of every move, his or her performance is in jeopardy.

Neurologist Scott Grafton of the University of Southern California in Los Angeles hypothesizes that performance failure sometimes occurs when the brain's fight-or-flight response overwhelms the brain, sending conflicting signals to the muscles. That might explain instances of what the sports world calls "choking"—as, for example, when a pole vaulter refuses to even come down the runway or a pro basketball player, shooting a critical free throw, misses everything, igniting the crowd's derisive chants of "Airball! Airball!" But what is happening when average golfers, during a leisurely game, consistently miss the three-foot putts they consistently make in practice? Is that true choking? James Fixx, who popularized running with his 1977 book *The Complete Book of Running*, described choking as "nothing more than an inability to relax when we take a match too seriously."

As Garfield observes, taking something too seriously, which is often described as a state of overarousal or being too "psyched up," is usually an enemy of peak performance. Although the animal-like pregame rituals of some football players—head butting, screaming, fighting—apparently are encouraged by some coaches, such behavior would be considered counterproductive in quarterbacks, whose emotional and intellectual stability is required for winning.

Still, the question remains: How does one "let go"? There is no single answer. American golf professional Jane Blalock has said, "I go into the locker room and find a corner by myself and just sit there. I try to achieve a peaceful state of nothingness that will carry over onto the golf course." Other athletes try to accomplish this state through prayer and Bible reading, listening to music, playing cards, or engaging in playful pranks before competition, all in an effort to loosen up and be relaxed. Martial arts icon Bruce Lee used mental imagery when trying to remove negative thoughts: "When such a thought enters my mind, I visualize it as being written on a piece of paper. Then I visualize myself wadding the paper into a tight ball. Then I mentally light it on fire and visualize it burning to a crisp. The negative thought is destroyed, never to enter my mind again."

Skiers, says sport psychologist Dan Gould of the University of North Carolina at Chapel Hill, are highly eclectic in their preparatory techniques. "For some of them, the mental preparation routine is very precise: They stretch; they imagine the course in their head; they think certain thoughts. Others shoot the breeze, do high-fives, and then get focused. What's interesting is that different athletes do it differently."

Timothy Gallwey is almost mystical in describing the process of avoiding negativism and achieving flow in the performance: "Letting go means allowing joy to come into your life instead of contriving to have a good time; learning to appreciate the love and beauty already happening around you rather than trying to manufacture something which you think isn't there; letting problems be solved in the unconscious mind as well as by straining with conscious effort."

While such advice no doubt has its value, Csikszentmihalyi and other researchers have attempted to put the concept of flow on a more solid footing. Their key point is that, for flow to occur, an athlete's perceived skills and the perceived demands of the sport situation must be in balance. When balance is absent, anxiety or boredom

occurs: anxiety if the athlete perceives the challenges as too great, boredom if the athlete's skills are much more than sufficient for the task. To truly experience flow, the athlete needs to feel stretched to the limit—but not beyond. The issue of perception is all-important. Researchers Susan Jackson and Glyn Roberts note: "A critical aspect of the flow situation is that the state of flow does not depend on the objective nature of the challenges present or on the objective nature of the skills of the individual. Whether one is in flow or not depends entirely on one's perceptions of the challenges and skills."

Beyond that essential matter of balance, the flow state, according to Csikszentmihalyi and other investigators, has the following characteristics:

—The merging of action and awareness. As Csikszentmihalyi expresses it: "People become so involved in what they are doing that the activity becomes spontaneous, almost automatic; they stop being aware of themselves as separate from the actions they are performing."

—Clear goals and unambiguous feedback. The athlete must have a clear idea of what he or she wants to accomplish and how the performance

is progressing toward that goal.

—Concentration on the task. The athlete shuts out distractions and focuses totally on the performance; activity and awareness are merged.

—The paradox of control. Csikszentmihalyi speaks of flow as involving "a sense of control—or, more precisely, as lacking the sense of worry about losing control that is typical in many situations of normal life."

—The loss of self-consciousness. Concern for the self vanishes; all attention is directed to the task.

—The transformation of time. As British runner Roger Bannister observed, the flow experience distorts time; the clock seems to either speed up or slow down.

Investigations of the flow state indicate that it is most likely to occur when athletes are oriented toward mastery of their sport rather than toward doing better than the competition. In contrast to coaches who emphasize the importance of wanting to win, flow theorists suggest that attaining the optimal energy zone—and therefore performing optimally—tends to occur, in the words of one researcher, when "the goal is not to be better than someone else but to do the best one can within the achievement situation."

Athletes say it best of all. "My best performance was when it seemed that my body and mind were in perfect unison," says a gymnast quoted in one important flow study. "There were no distractions. It was just myself and the event. Winning was not important." Moreover, this athlete added, "It was not an exhausting experience as it sometimes is. It was energizing."

Change and innovation are as evident in the physical preparation of top athletes as on the mental front.

Far more attention is now paid to year-round training and muscle flexibility than was the case only a few years ago, and work with weights is much more widespread. For example, basketball players used to avoid lifting weights for fear that it would add muscle bulk, which is not particularly desired in a sport that requires quickness, leaping ability, and touch. Now,

however, the NBA's best players employ a moderate amount of weightlifting throughout their grueling season to maintain endurance. Their technique is to do many repetitions of relatively low weight, rather than a few major lifts of greater weight.

Some coaches have developed highly unorthodox training routines. Mike Powell, world-record holder in

In a high-tech workout, three Denver Bronco football players run against the resistance of drag parachutes attached to their belts. Conceived by a Soviet track coach, the chutes not only help to improve players' speed, acceleration, and endurance but also encourage proper running technique. Their use has spread to other sports, including ice hockey and basketball.

Recuperating from surgery on his left knee, German ski jumper Jens Weissflogg—1984 Olympic champion in the 70-meter event— uses a ramp, skateboard, and foam-rubber landing area to get ready for the 1992 games. At the top level of sports today, conditioning and skill sharpening are a nonstop affair.

the long jump, attributes much of his success to a five-year training program designed by his coach, Randy Huntington, whose fondness for new training techniques has earned him the nickname Mr. Gizmo. On training days, Powell often works to build explosive power in his legs by running on the track with an open drag parachute trailing behind him. To reduce the risk of injury and shorten the recovery time needed between workouts, Powell frequently exercises in a pool. He also stimulates his muscles by applying low currents of electricity with a battery-operated device.

In resistance, or strength, training, athletes are focusing more on the development of specific muscles that tests have shown will aid their performance. Not long ago, world-class cyclists trained almost exclusively by the most obvious method: riding their bikes. Now, however, they are giving more attention to their hamstrings, a group of muscles in the back of the thigh, because these muscles stabilize the knee and transfer mechanical energy between the joints. Similarly, swimmers now work to build up their arms, because computer analysis has shown that about 80 percent of their propulsion through the water comes from arm movement. (An added psychological benefit to these new training regimens is that they offer a change in scenery and routine from

the long hours in the pool, on the track, or on a bicycle. Breaking the monotony of training, which can sap the spirit of even the most determined athlete, has always been a goal of innovative coaches.)

Some of the most productive work on the physical side of sport is being done by biomechanists, who view athletes with an engineer's eye. As Charles Dillman, formerly of the U.S. Olympic Training Center, has put it, "We look at the human body as if it were a machine. For us, muscles and limbs are pulleys and levers with their own measurable moments of inertia and torque. For every motion in each sport, we hope to find something close to an optimal movement of the body, whether it be the most efficient way a hockey player can accelerate on the ice or the maximum torso rotation over the high-jump bar."

Nowadays, biomechanists seem to contribute to virtually every world-class athletic performance, from rowing to weightlifting to ski jumping. By using high-speed video of up to 200 frames per second, they are able to create three-dimensional stick figures that detail the position, velocity, and acceleration of all parts of the body. They have improved the stroke of

swimmers after learning that the hand can propel more water if the fingers are slightly separated, like a duck's webbed foot. They have identified the best angle for javelin throwers to release the spear.

Bicyclists have been major beneficiaries of biomechanical analysis. Many top United States cyclists have worked with biomechanist Jefferey Broker, who uses videotapes and computers to measure the motion of an athlete's limbs. "Within a couple of hours of videotaping," Broker notes, the computers can produce "a full stick figure of the cyclist on the bicycle. We then have programs that look at the stick-figure motion and apply the forces that we measure at the pedal to the foot for the stick figure."

Similar analysis is carried out for forces at the hip, knee, and ankle, according to Broker, "so we can get a sense of what muscle groups are involved and where the power is being developed within the musculoskeletal system and then finally delivered to the bicycle." In the end, the cyclist may adjust his or her position on the bike. Says Broker, "We may have a rider who is extremely fast or is capable of producing large power outputs but has high frontal drag because of the position of his trunk. We may be able to change his position to make him more aerodynamic without negatively affecting his power."

Participating in a 100-mile ultramarathon across steep Southwestern terrain in 1993, Tarahumara Indians from Mexico's Sierra Madre demonstrate their seemingly boundless physical reserves. Running games are a major cultural activity for Tarahumara of all ages. This contest was won by Victoriano Churro *(top)*—at 55, the oldest participant ever to finish first.

layed by radio signals to a laptop computer on the coach's boat, and the coach can assemble it in various ways just by tapping the computer's touch-screen menu. For example, if the coach was monitoring the performance of an eight-person boat and wanted to see what was happening on the boat's right side alone, he could call for graphlike traces representing the oarlock force for each oar (and each separate oar pull) on that side of the boat. He could also superimpose the traces—in different colors—to compare the right-side performances of the eight rowers.

Devices such as this one, called the Data Acquisition System (DAS), may well find their way into many other types of sports. Sensors could give trainers information on a boxer's every punch; coaches could know in-

The aspirations of biomechanists seem to know no bounds. At the Olympic Training Center, they are perfecting an extraordinarily sophisticated training device for rowers. It will use as many as 160 sensors to generate a real-time profile of a rowing performance during a practice session. Among other things, the sensors will measure the relative wind and water velocity, the acceleration or deceleration of the boat, the angles of the oars, the forces applied to the oars and foot stretchers, and even the rower's heart rate.

All of this information will be re-

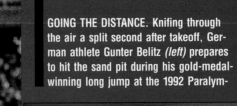

GOING THE DISTANCE. Knifing through the air a split second after takeoff, German athlete Gunter Belitz *(left)* prepares to hit the sand pit during his gold-medal-winning long jump at the 1992 Paralympics in Barcelona. Belitz, whose left leg was amputated more than 20 years ago, competes with a customized prosthetic limb. He set a new world record in his class with this 4.82-meter effort.

A Winning State of Mind

Athletes of every stripe benefit from the equipment they use. But it takes more than a pair of high-tech running shoes to make a top-ranked competitor. Indeed, it even takes more than physical prowess—a fact that is perhaps most clearly demonstrated at the Paralympic Games, the quadrennial gathering for the world's most outstanding disabled athletes. Although some of these individuals could not perform without the aid of their prosthetic devices, what defines them as top-ranked athletes are the same intangible qualities that drive their able-bodied counterparts: a desire to compete and a will to win that pushes both mind and body to the limit.

Paralympic contestants come from several large groups: amputees, the visually impaired, paraplegics and quadriplegics, people with cerebral palsy, and others. Events parallel some of those in the traditional Olympics, from track and field to swimming, but each of the 15 or so sports is subdivided into classes that reflect the different degrees of disability among the competitors. For example, wheelchair racers (*far left*) compete in four categories based on amount of upper-body mobility, from those with full movement to those who have the use of only their arms and hands.

In some cases, records set at the Paralympics, which are held a few weeks after the Summer Olympics at the same site, come astoundingly close to the best Olympic marks. In 1988, for example, the winner of the men's high jump, who has only one leg, cleared the bar at just over two meters, less than half a meter short of the world record at the time.

Beyond any obvious physical features, coaches and other observers often find it difficult to distinguish Paralympians from Olympians in such areas as commitment to training. As for the athletes themselves, most are so focused on excelling that their disability never even enters their mind.

STRIDE FOR STRIDE. Tony Volpentest *(inset, left)* exhibits the form and speed that won him two gold medals and established Paralympic world track records at Barcelona. Born without hands or feet and running with carbon-graphite limbs, the 21-year-old American finished the 100-meter sprint in 11.63 seconds—less than two seconds shy of the current Olympic world record. His coach describes him as the most impressive athlete she has ever trained in her 25-year career.

stantly if a luge team was banking too high on curves or if a runner was leaning too much. The possibilities seem boundless, promising a level of physical understanding of performance that would have seemed magical to coaches only a generation ago.

Many of the challenges faced by top athletes have parallels in other professional fields—in the performing arts or in business, for instance. As anxiety inducing as shooting a critical free throw in front of 20,000 people may be, it can hardly exceed the pressures of performing a solo at the Metropolitan Opera.

The road to success for tenors, violinists, and actors is every bit as stressful as the Olympic athlete's. Cutthroat competition and pressure from parents and coaches may begin as early as grade school, and, if anything, it is likely to increase. Some may develop almost paralyzing anxiety as they face a performance. Even those who demonstrate technical brilliance and achieve a degree of stardom are not immune to the pressures.

Actress Glenda Jackson, much acclaimed for her work in the theater as well as in cinema, has said that by late afternoon on performance days she can feel the butterflies coming on; later, as she applies her stage makeup, her fingers tremble and palms begin to sweat. As the curtain rises,

her heart pounds, and she finds herself thinking, "I simply can't go on." But, of course, she does. Internationally known pianist Josef Lhevinne was often so nervous that his wife, Rosina, would have to push him onstage. Vladimir Horowitz and Arthur Rubinstein admitted that, even quite late in their careers, they were nerv-

ous before every performance. For every one of these stories, there are other tales of talented people who never reached their full potential because of a traumatic fear of failure. They opened their mouths or poised their fingers above the keys and not a sound was made.

Glen Gabbard, a staff psychiatrist at the Menninger Clinic in Topeka, Kansas (and a professional actor and singer in his own right), cites "the fear of narcissistic injury" as the basis for

A young dancer waits in the wings for her cue. Many performers must overcome fear of failure every time they go onstage. World-famous pianist William Kapell wrote, "The first ten minutes of every concert are lost to me, while I get accustomed all over again to being there."

garden-variety stage fright. In plain words, performers are prey to anxiety —sometimes overwhelming anxiety— because they feel that their worth as a person is directly tied to their performance. The possibility of failure poses a severe threat to their self-esteem, and a desire to avoid the situation is a natural response. Mental imagery of

successful, reassuring scenes helps some people to overcome these moments. A soprano who also happens to be a young mother might want to practice her solo as a nighttime lullaby for her child; although it may not induce sleep as well as a traditional tune, the warm, pleasurable experience can be immediately recalled later when she is standing before that cold, cruel audience.

Some psychologists recommend systematic campaigns against performance anxiety. Donald Meichenbaum, professor of psychology at the University of Waterloo in Ontario, Canada, has devised a program called Stress Inoculation Training that helps performers to become aware of the source of stress and to develop and apply effective coping skills. Meichenbaum's program involves relaxation training and mental imagery, and it also requires performers to make an honest assessment of the attitudes and beliefs that underlie their nervousness. For example, some performers secretly fear being unmasked as frauds, even if they are widely respected by their peers; others believe that one bad performance will unravel a career of quality work. Both fears are usually irrational and—when brought into the open and honestly faced—can be expunged.

This so-called cognitive restructuring is a gradual process. The "inocula-

tion" element of Meichenbaum's program entails exposure to small, manageable amounts of stress that will stimulate, rather than overwhelm, the coping skills that the performer is endeavoring to master.

Cognitive tools can be useful in business, too. For example, the Metropolitan Life Insurance Company offers its sales personnel a program described as "optimism training." Explains one company official, "Our people do a lot of cold-calling. After 20 calls, they may have only one interested client. Optimism training gives them a sort of immunity to all the turndowns." The program is designed to teach appropriate responses when things go badly—avoiding self-blame, realizing that the effects of a mistake are likely to be only temporary, and keeping work problems separate from other areas of life. The business world is also making increasing use of imaging techniques. Top performers, notes Charles Garfield, sometimes give themselves an extremely demanding goal and then mentally focus on a picture of themselves meeting it.

In any field where performance pressures are great—sports, the arts, business—it is all too easy to lose sight of the biggest picture of all, the

ultimate victory of leading a full, emotionally satisfying life. When anything, whether marathons or model airplanes, so dominates our days that we have no time for love, laughter, or aimless walks in the woods, what have we accomplished with our sophisticated relaxation techniques? When obsessive training for medals leaves no time for family and friends, what is the medal worth?

In the fall of 1993, Chinese women distance runners obliterated world records in the 1,500, 3,000, and 10,000 meters. Amid worldwide speculation that they were using performance-enhancing drugs—a charge vehemently denied—their coach claimed that some of them trained as much as 180 miles a week. That works out to a marathon a day, a training schedule that most of the world's running community would deem foolhardy and injurious (and perhaps impossible).

The Chinese exploits evoked memories of the former Soviet-bloc sport programs in which athletic four-year-olds were taken from their families and pushed onto a steroidal road meant to lead to Olympic stardom.

For many, the road was a dead end: They failed or lost interest and were cast out of the training programs, their lives no longer of consequence to the coaches and trainers who had been

their de facto parents. Even some of those who won national glory and worldwide fame came to bitterly regret missing a normal childhood.

It could be said that the very notion of sport is called into question by efforts to create superathletes. As one author puts it, "The viewer is no longer watching a celebration of

The Plight of a
Keyboard Superstar

Just as athletes risk injury by placing extreme demands on their bodies, musicians are prone to problems with the muscles and tendons that they use (and often overuse) to operate their instruments. Surveys suggest that at least half of them experience difficulties severe enough to jeopardize their careers. The renowned concert pianist Gary Graffman is one who had to confront such a calamity. In 1979 he found himself hitting wrong notes with his right hand in difficult passages. He tried to ignore the mistakes, but his control grew worse. After a five-month odyssey of medical consultations, the reason for the errant play was finally pinned down: Because of a fingering change he had made several years earlier to compensate for a sprain, the extensor muscles on his ring and little fingers had become so weak that they curled involuntarily. Doctors described the ailment as an "overuse syndrome."

Although no cure proved possible, Graffman has continued with his performing career, playing pieces composed for the left hand alone. He has also openly discussed his ordeal, drawing attention to the medical problems of musicians. With recognition has come help. Today, many cities have special clinics for musician-patients.

human potential but rather a kind of freak show." Still, the quest for ever higher levels of performance is unlikely to abate. Records will continue to fall, and some of them may fall far. For example, Jay Kearney, a physiologist in the Sport Science Division of the U.S. Olympic Committee, predicts that the track record for the mile, currently three minutes 44 seconds, will drop some 10 seconds by the middle of the 21st century.

In the years ahead, sport psychology will no doubt enlarge its present kit of imagery, biofeedback, and other mind-enlisting techniques. Biomechanics is certain to extend its analytic reach with more powerful computers, better sensors, and improved software. The winner's edge will thus be an ever moving frontier. It is to be hoped, though, that the new appreciation of the mind in sports will help keep that edge in perspective.

Mihaly Csikszentmihalyi frames the issue in terms of his concept of optimal experience: "To get the most out of sports either as a participant or as a spectator, one should be able to enjoy the activity for its own sake, regardless of the outcome. That is what flow is all about."

Long-distance swimmer and triathlete Julie Ridge sees performance in even more broad terms. In words that would surely find widespread agreement throughout the world of sports and beyond, she writes: "Just putting yourself on the line, commanding your mind or your body to perform, and giving your best effort is a celebration of yourself, of your capabilities, of being alive."

THE WINNING EDGE

The tape stretches taut, then snaps as an Olympic sprinter leans into the finish, his nearest opponent less than an inch behind him. At a pool nearby, two swimmers racing neck and neck tap underwater touch pads fractions of a second apart. In both events, the competitors are so close together that the human eye cannot tell the winner; only sophisticated electronic instruments can accurately gauge their times.

For elite athletes, the difference between a gold medal and no medal at all is often measured in just millimeters and hundredths of seconds. In this realm of excellence where competitors are nearly indistinguishable in skill and ability, each must make use of any advantage that might bridge the sometimes infinitesimal gap between first and second place. Now, many world-class athletes are turning to science to help them make such incremental improvements and tap the hidden mental and physical stores they need to win.

Researchers are finding that achieving peak performance depends on a unique blend of mental training, physical conditioning, and technique. By studying the effects of these ingredients on an individual's performance and determining how the mixture can be altered to improve scores and times, sport scientists in the fields of psychology, physiology, and biomechanics are working together to help coaches perfect the ways their athletes train and compete.

Proof of their success, and of the seemingly limitless capabilities of the mind and body, becomes increasingly clear as world records continue to fall and as human beings routinely accomplish what was once called impossible.

VISIONS OF VICTORY

For today's athlete, the mind must be as well trained as the body. Such psychic conditioning is the province of sport psychologists, who study thought processes that encourage peak performance and develop customized mental skills that athletes must practice just as they would any physical exercise. Much of sport psychology's current focus is stress management: dealing with the intense strain of training and competition.

To master stress, athletes are taught to control their level of mental excitement, or "energy." Research suggests a zone of optimal functioning for every individual. Above this energy level, the athlete may "choke," or lose composure; below it, he or she may fall short of the goal.

People can gain control over these levels well before competition, and even on the starting line, with the aid of special psychological tools. Mental imagery—visualizing, say, power being drawn from spectators or opponents—can help bring on a surge of needed energy. To dispel unwanted energy, athletes can turn to relaxation training, involving techniques such as controlled breathing and the association of certain words or thoughts with a calm state.

Athletes use a number of other strategies for mastering stress. One is to establish a set routine, such as always warming up the same way or mentally performing an event before it actually begins. To direct their training constructively, athletes learn to set specific, short-term, achievable goals—improving speed off the starting line, for example—rather than focusing only on the outcome, such as winning the gold.

EXERCISING THE MIND. Mentally rehearsing her event, a skier *(left)* leans into an imagined turn. Like many athletes, she combines two types of imagery: Using internal imagery, she visualizes the scene—including such details as her ski tips rushing downhill *(below)*—as it might unfold before her eyes; external imagery provides a view of her actions from an observer's perspective *(right)*. Athletes use visualization to practice new skills, correct problems with form, or "preview" a flawless performance.

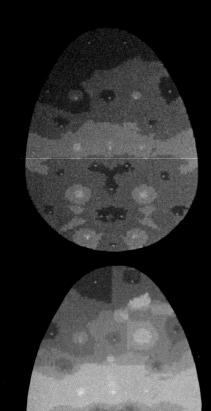

CATCHING THE FLOW. Many athletes, such as the archer above, strive for the trancelike "flow state," in which performance seems effortless. Composite readings of the mental activity of 12 archers revealed in the pair of brain scans below suggest that this elusive state has a physiological link. Subtle dabs of color in the upper image indicate the relatively low brain activity of the athletes in simple repose. The lower image, by contrast, shows what happens when the archers visualize the act of shooting. Bright yellow bursts of low-frequency alpha waves denote an active but relaxed state in brain areas concerned with planning and fine movements.

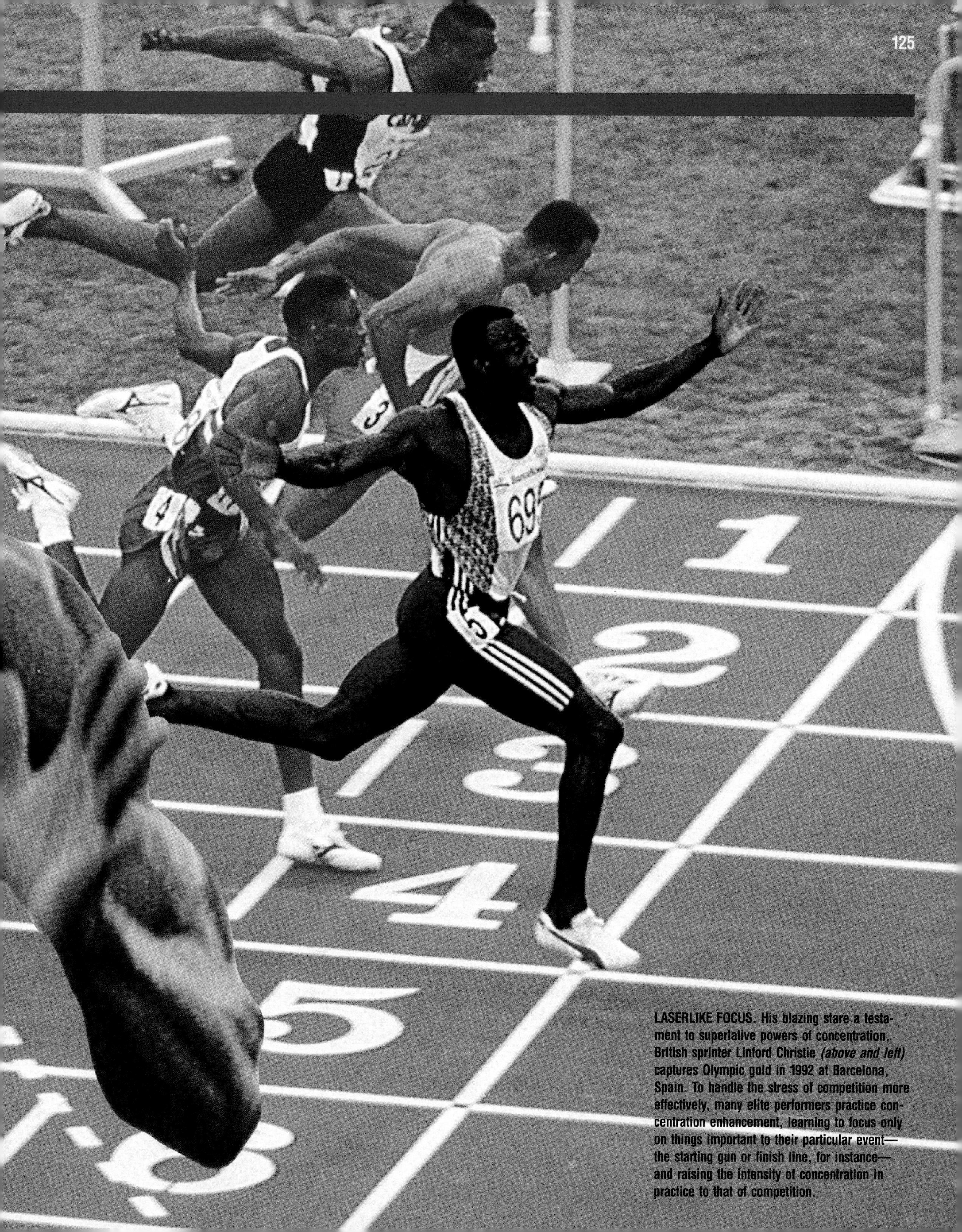

LASERLIKE FOCUS. His blazing stare a testament to superlative powers of concentration, British sprinter Linford Christie *(above and left)* captures Olympic gold in 1992 at Barcelona, Spain. To handle the stress of competition more effectively, many elite performers practice concentration enhancement, learning to focus only on things important to their particular event— the starting gun or finish line, for instance— and raising the intensity of concentration in practice to that of competition.

TUNING THE MACHINE

By studying the demands of different sports and how the human body reacts to training over time, sport physiologists can develop customized programs that improve responses and hone an athlete's competitive edge.

Each sport requires a distinct approach. For endurance events, such as distance running, physiologists focus on the ways athletes produce energy by using oxygen. Researchers often monitor respiration, for example, because of the vital role oxygen plays in generating energy.

Another test determines the levels of lactate, a by-product of energy production, circulating in the blood. (In the muscles, where it is produced, the substance is called lactic acid.) Certain types of training have been found to promote lower lactate levels, which researchers have linked to better performance in endurance events. Heart rate is also a good indicator of energy production, because a particular rate suggests a specific level of oxygen use and lactate production.

In sports such as weightlifting and sprinting, which depend less on oxygen for energy, physiologists focus on other areas of the body. Using special equipment, they monitor specific muscle groups—a sprinter's upper legs, for instance—to see if training is increasing strength and explosive power. If not, the training can be changed. Scientists hope that physiological research will prove yet more valuable to athletes. One possible innovation: a way to identify overtraining through analysis of hormone levels.

MEASURED BREATHS. Stroking to stay apace in an artificial current, a swimmer in an underwater treadmill *(above)* breathes through a snorkel-like device. At left, researchers on a golf cart use a similar instrument, attached to a weather balloon, to collect exhaled air from a runner. Air samples from the lungs of athletes in action help determine the amount of oxygen used at various levels of exertion. Intake during an all-out effort reveals the body's aerobic power, or maximum ability to consume oxygen for producing energy. Readings at lesser speeds show the efficiency of oxygen use at specific paces. Sport physiologists take frequent readings during various types of training to help athletes determine which exercises, intensities, and paces are most beneficial. Even slight improvements in aerobic power or efficiency can greatly reduce the effort required to maintain a given speed—meaning that the athlete should be able to cover the same distance in less time.

ELEMENTS OF STYLE

Though it hints of space-age cyborgs and robots, sport biomechanics is a down-to-earth way of exploring the dynamics of human movement. Simply put, scientists in this field analyze nuances of an athlete's performance and suggest changes in technique that are designed to save time, increase power, and prevent injury.

For their analysis of any sport, biomechanists first use high-speed video cameras to record an athlete's movements. Then they feed this footage into a computer that converts human forms into three-dimensional stick figures, which can be animated and observed, frame by frame, from any angle. The shapes are ideal for studying the orientation and position of arms, legs, trunk, and equipment during critical moments of a performance—details that are often too fleeting to be grasped by the eye alone. The system computes angles, positions, velocities, and accelerations of each moving part and, hooked to other devices, can measure the force being applied by the hands and feet. This allows scientists to determine, say, if a weightlifter is applying equal force with each leg as he pushes upward.

Such information is useful not only for evaluating individual style but also for spotting slight variations in form—the way a swimmer cocks a hand or a cyclist pushes on the pedals—that may promote or detract from economy of movement. Far more effective than formulas on a blackboard, the stick figures serve as a powerful tool for scientists trying to explain their findings to athletes and coaches. And a new generation of computer programs has emerged, offering uncannily realistic graphics and an even closer look at the intricacies of movement.

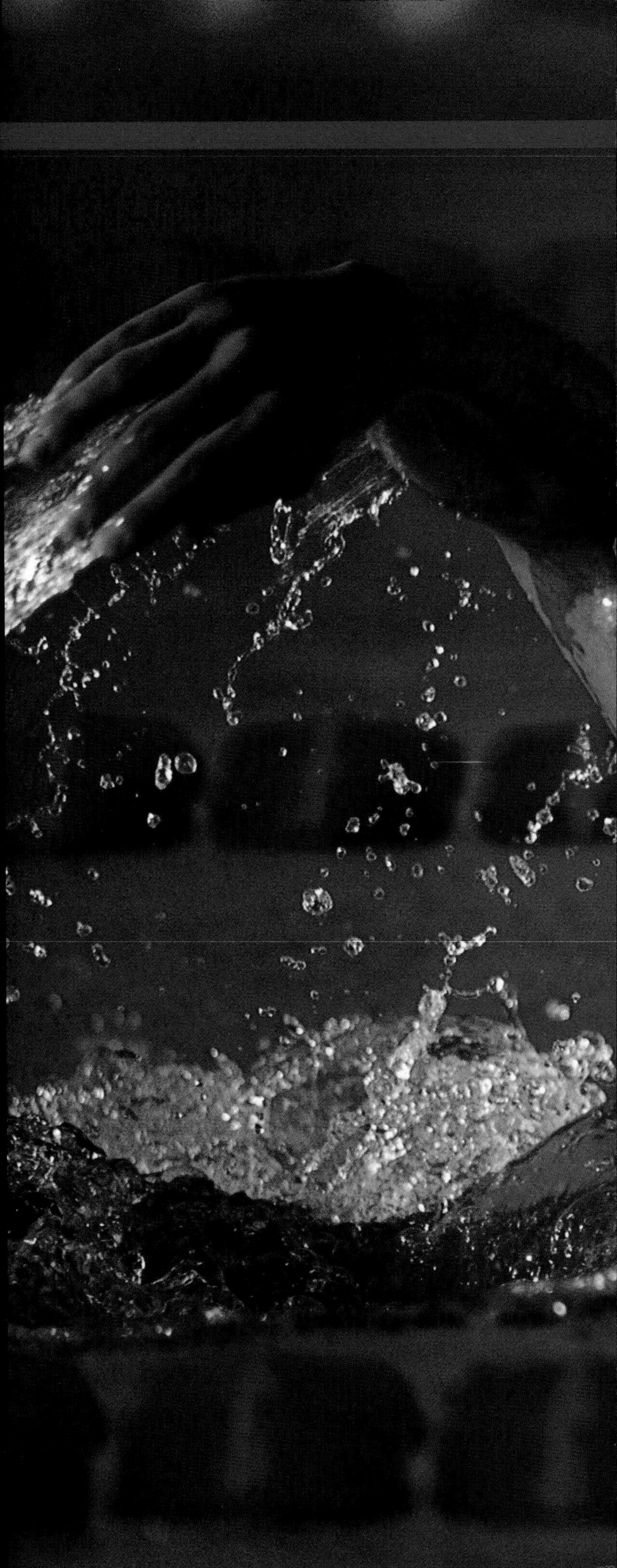

HIGH-TECH COACHING. As a swimmer speeds through the water *(below)*, a computer helps convert the videotaped movements into graphic form. At right, three high-tech images of the stroke—viewed simultaneously from the front, side, and below—show the motions of the body and, for purposes of analysis, right arm only. Sport biomechanists study the images in fine detail, tracing the hand's path during the stroke *(indicated by a banded line)* while plotting the amount of force it exerts along the way *(graph at bottom)*. On the graph, the large gap between the hand's total force *(top wavy line)* and the amount used to propel the body through the water *(bottom wavy line)* tells biomechanists that the athlete is wasting energy in the first part of the stroke. The scientists' advice: Streamline the hand's entry and increase the arm's outward sweep.

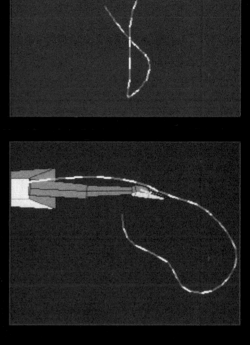

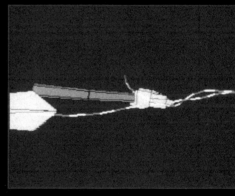

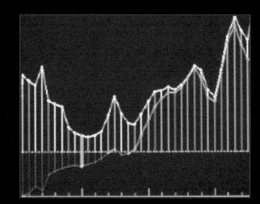

STEADY HANDS. Biomechanics can capture subtleties in a weightlifter's routine that escape the naked eye. In the computer image below, stick figures represent key movements during the critical moment when the athlete jerks the barbell *(white dash)* off the floor and above his head. The blue line snaking through the body tracks the lifter's center of gravity. Below the stick figure, a graph plots the speeds, in millimeters per second, of the left and right sides of the barbell *(red and blue lines, respectively)*. The lines split halfway through the maneuver, indicating that the bar is not level. To compensate, the athlete used strength that might have been applied to lifting more weight.

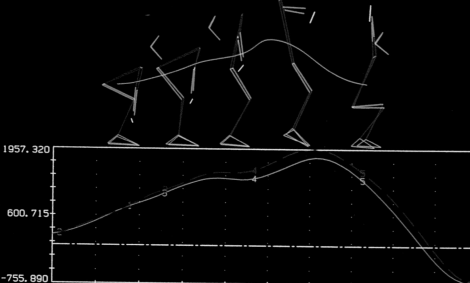

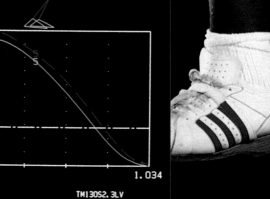

WINNING FORM. Stick-figure sequences of two athletes hurling a javelin *(below)* provide an excellent way for sport scientists to compare techniques. The thrower in the top sequence holds the javelin low with a notable upward tilt. At the moment of release *(third figure from right)*, the grip creates a steep angle between the javelin's center *(path traced by red line)* and its tip—causing drag and sapping distance from the throw. The athlete at bottom, however, holds the javelin high and relatively flat, releasing it at a shallower angle that makes its flight more aerodynamic. The result: a longer throw.

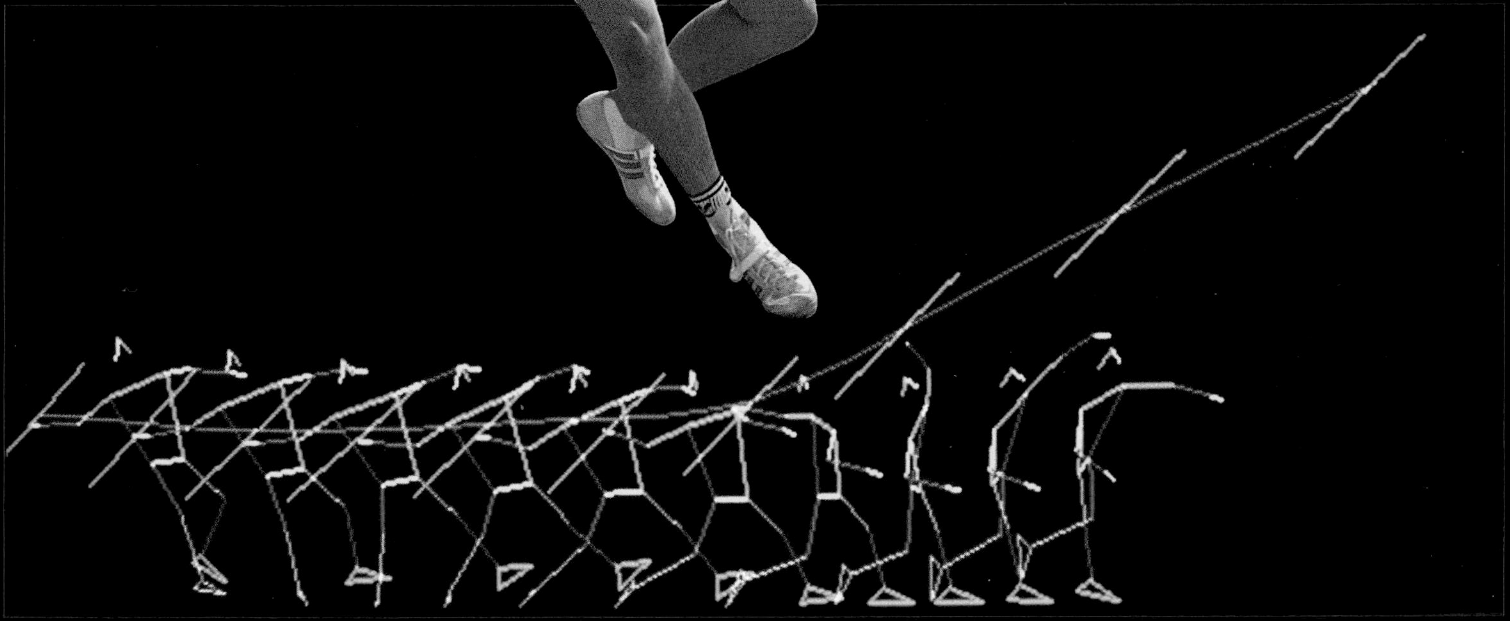

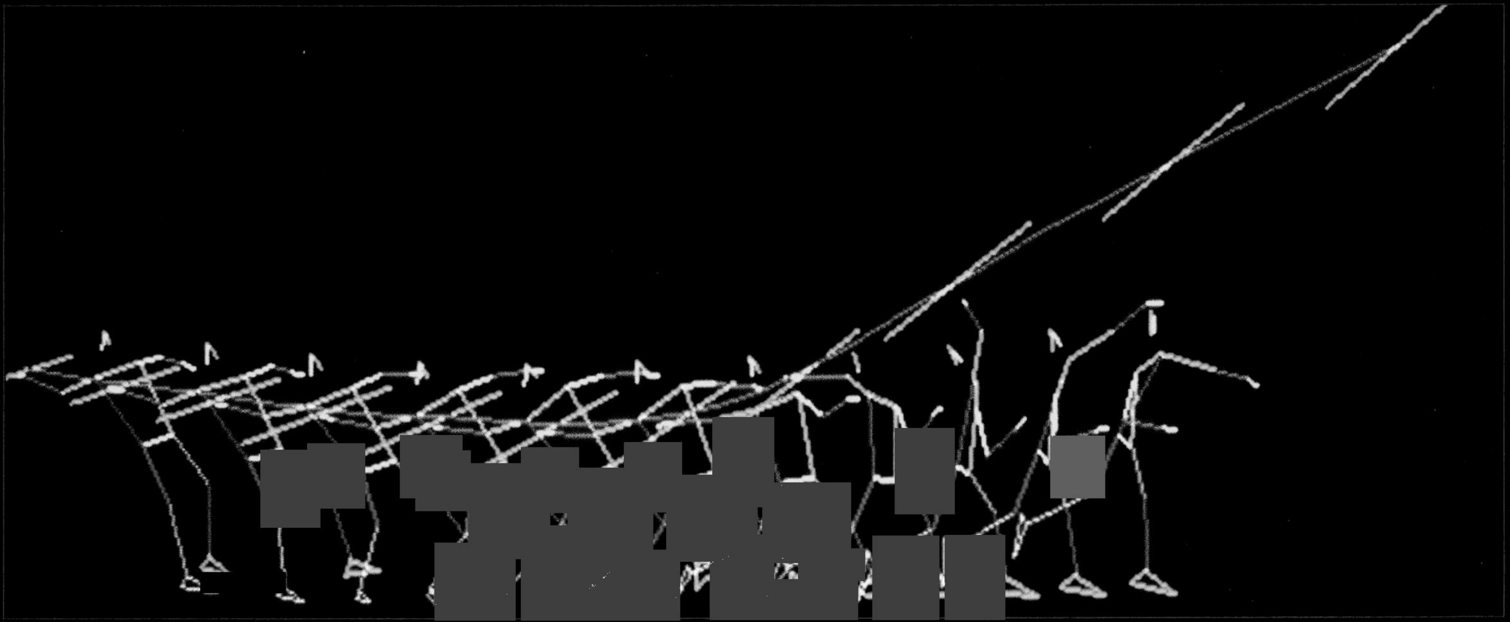

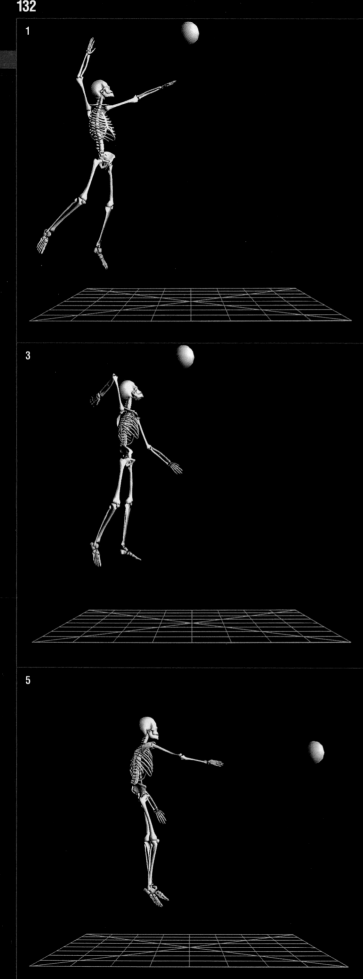

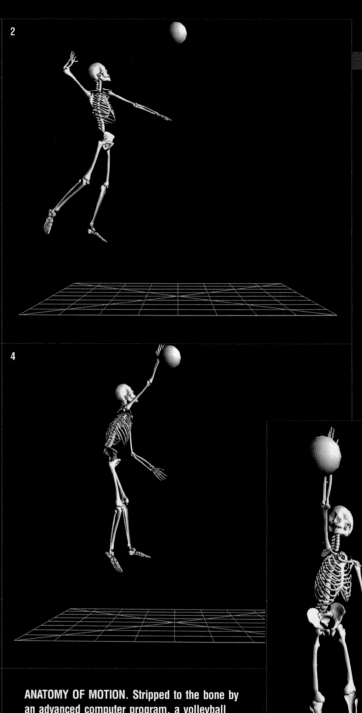

ANATOMY OF MOTION. Stripped to the bone by an advanced computer program, a volleyball player leaps to spike the ball in a vivid biomechanical sequence. Each image rotates to any angle, as shown by the frontal view at right. The next evolutionary step above stick figures, skeletal models such as these are more faithful to actual movement.

VIRTUALLY REAL. By "fleshing out" the skeletal images, researchers can create eerily realistic models, such as the baseball player at right, that are proportionally identical to the actual athlete. The latest computer programs can echo parts of the action—here, the bat and ball—with stroboscopic afterimages that allow closer scrutiny of specific movements.

GLOSSARY

Acetylcholine (ACh): a neurotransmitter that, among other things, causes inhibition of the heart rate, initiates muscle contractions, and stimulates the adrenal glands. ACh plays an important role in maintaining the initial reactions of the stress response.

Acupuncture: an ancient Chinese medical procedure that involves insertion of fine needles at specific points of the body. Acupuncture is used both to treat illness and to induce anesthesia.

Adrenal glands: two small glands, located just above the kidneys, that consist of two parts: the cortex, or outer layer, which produces steroid hormones; and the medulla, or inner portion, which produces the hormones epinephrine and norepinephrine.

Adrenaline: *See* Epinephrine.

Alarm reaction: *See* General adaptation syndrome.

Alpha waves: electrical activity of the brain, as measured by an electroencephalograph, during a state of relaxed wakefulness, characterized by frequencies of about eight to 13 hertz, or cycles per second.

Amino acids: a class of chemical compounds that are the building blocks of proteins; various combinations of about 20 basic amino acids make up all the proteins in the human body.

Anabolic steroids: synthetic hormones that help increase muscle bulk and strength. Anabolic steroids can have several detrimental side effects, including liver damage and violent behavior.

Analgesia: loss of a sense of pain.

Anxiety: mental distress caused by the anticipation of threat or danger. Anxiety can have several physiological effects, such as increased heart rate and sweating.

Autonomic nervous system: the system of nerves that regulates normally involuntary bodily processes, such as blood pressure, heart rate, breathing, and digestion. Part of the peripheral nervous system, the autonomic nervous system consists of sympathetic and parasympathetic divisions. *See also* Parasympathetic nervous system, Peripheral nervous system, Sympathetic nervous system.

Biofeedback: a technique in which an individual learns to control a normally involuntary function such as blood pressure by responding to information, or feedback, about that function supplied by a monitoring device. Biofeedback is often used as a method of learning how to reach a state of relaxation.

Brainstem: the part of the brain that is continuous with the top of the spinal cord. The brainstem consists of the medulla, the midbrain, and the pons, and is involved in the routing of all incoming and outgoing nerve signals.

Brain waves: fluctuations in the electrical activity of many brain cells as recorded by an electroencephalograph.

Central nervous system: the part of the nervous system consisting of the brain and spinal cord.

Cerebral cortex: the thin outer layer of the cerebrum in mammals. The cortex is responsible for higher brain functions such as learning, thought, and memory.

Chromaffin cells: cells that have an affinity for chrome salt stains. In the adrenal medulla, such cells secrete epinephrine and norepinephrine.

Cortisol: one of the steroid hormones produced by the cortex of the adrenal gland. Cortisol plays an important role in the stress response by, among other things, promoting the production of glucose to supply energy.

Dopamine: a neurotransmitter involved in the regulation of emotion, movement, and the perception of pain.

Dorsal horn: part of the soft gray matter of the spinal cord that relays pain signals and other sensory nerve impulses to the brain.

Electroencephalograph: a device that monitors the electrical signals given off by neurons firing in the cerebral cortex.

Endocrine system: the body's network of glands and other organs that secrete hormones.

Endorphin: any of a class of molecules, produced naturally in the brain and in other tissues, that bind to the brain's opiate receptors; endorphins thus can act as

painkillers and can induce a euphoric state of mind.

Enkephalin: an opioid, produced in the brain, that consists of a chain of five amino acids; from the Greek for "in the head." Enkephalin has an analgesic effect.

Epinephrine: a stress-related hormone, produced by the adrenal medulla, that increases heart rate, blood pressure, and carbohydrate metabolism; also known as adrenaline. Epinephrine is also produced by neurons and functions as a neurotransmitter.

Exhaustion stage: *See* General adaptation syndrome.

Fight-or-flight response: the central and sympathetic nervous systems' reaction to threat or stress, which quickly prepares the body for conflict or escape. *See also* General adaptation syndrome.

Flow: the elusive trancelike condition during an activity in which performance seems effortless and an individual is completely attentive to the task at hand and focused only on relevant cues from the environment.

Ganglion: a bundle or mass of nerve cells outside the brain or spinal cord. In the autonomic nervous system, ganglia serve as relay points for impulses traveling from the central nervous system to various target organs in the body.

Gate control theory: the theory that neuronal mechanisms in the spinal cord's dorsal horns can modify pain impulses traveling from the peripheral nervous system to the central nervous system.

General adaptation syndrome: a series of physical responses initiated by the hypothalamus in response to stress. The general adaptation syndrome includes three stages: the alarm reaction, during which the body is prepared for fight or flight; the resistance stage, during which the body tries to adapt to prolonged stress; and the exhaustion stage, when the body can no longer adapt. *See also* Fight-or-flight response.

Glucose: a simple sugar that is the major fuel source for cells.

Homeostasis: a condition of internal equilibrium, in which most of the body's processes function within limits set by the hypothalamus.

Hormones: chemicals released by glands and a few other organs that travel through the bloodstream and regulate the activities of specific tissues, organs, and other glands.

Hypothalamus: a structure in the brain that controls many autonomic functions, such as body temperature, and also produces hormones and neurotransmitters.

Immune system: a network of tissues, cells, and cell products that mobilizes against foreign substances, attacks infections, and removes debris from the body. The immune system includes the spleen, the thymus, lymph tissue and nodes, white blood cells, and antibodies.

Lactic acid: a waste product produced when muscles burn fuel. The buildup of lactic acid can cause muscle fatigue.

Limbic system: the collective term for several related structures in the brain that are involved in emotion, memory, and the regulation of certain autonomic functions.

Medulla: the lowest of the three segments of the brainstem, responsible for, among other things, the regulation of breathing and blood pressure; also, the center part of a gland or organ.

Mental imagery: a process of directed or guided meditation that uses mental images to promote or produce a desired response in the body; also known as visualization.

Mental rehearsal: the creation of mental images of the exact movements that an individual wishes to achieve in reality.

Midbrain: the uppermost of the three segments of the brainstem, serving primarily as an intermediary between the rest of the brain and the spinal cord.

Nervous system: the entire system of nerves and nerve centers in the body, including the brain, spinal cord, nerves, and ganglia.

Neuron: a nerve cell, consisting of a central body from which extend a number of branches called dendrites for receiving signals, and a single fiber called an axon

for transmitting signals; the human brain is made up of somewhere between 10 billion and 100 billion neurons.

Neurotransmitter: any of a number of chemical substances, synthesized by neurons, that are involved in the transmission of electrochemical impulses across the synaptic gap from one neuron to another or from a neuron to a muscle or gland.

Nociceptor: a pain-specific nerve ending; from the Latin for "to injure."

Norepinephrine: a hormone, produced by the adrenal medulla, that constricts blood vessels and raises blood pressure; also known as noradrenaline. Norepinephrine is also produced by neurons and functions as a neurotransmitter.

Opioid: an opiumlike substance. The term is often used to refer specifically to substances produced in the body and brain in response to stress. *See also* Endorphin, Enkephalin.

Oxygen debt: The amount of oxygen needed by the body to break down lactic acid accumulating in the muscles.

Parasympathetic nervous system: one of two divisions of the autonomic nervous system. The parasympathetic nervous system typically acts in balanced opposition to the sympathetic nervous system, functioning to bring the body back into homeostasis.

Peptide: a chain of amino acids with specific chemical bonds between the acids.

Periaqueductal gray (PAG): an area in the midbrain that contains narcotic receptors and can send pain-inhibiting messages to the spinal cord.

Peripheral nervous system: the nerves that extend from the spinal cord throughout the rest of the body. It has two subdivisions: the autonomic nervous system, made up of the nerves that regulate normally involuntary functions such as heart rate; and the somatic nervous system, made up of the nerves that control voluntary functions, such as walking.

Pituitary gland: a structure, located in the brain near the hypothalamus, that controls all other glands in the body through the release of hormones.

Pons: a section of the brainstem that links the cerebral cortex to the cerebellum.

Protein: a molecule consisting of amino acids linked together and folded to form a distinct shape that determines the protein's function. Proteins are the fundamental components of the body and play an essential role in all biological processes.

Resistance reaction: *See* General adaptation syndrome.

Reticular formation: a network of neurons, extending from the spinal cord through the brainstem and into the cerebrum, that may be involved in virtually every aspect of nervous system function.

Spinal cord: a thick cable of nerves and associated nerve cells, housed within the backbone, that relays impulses between the brain and the rest of the body; the spinal cord and the brain form the central nervous system.

Spleen: a lymphoid organ in the abdomen that serves as a filter for blood, a production site for antibodies, and the body's major site for dismantling worn red blood cells.

Stress: the body's response to an external or internal circumstance that disturbs normal equilibrium.

Stressor: a stimulus that leads to stress.

Sympathetic nervous system: one of two divisions of the autonomic nervous system. The sympathetic nervous system stimulates the body, preparing it for fight or flight.

Thalamus: a structure within the brain that initially processes all sensory input except smell and routes it to the cerebral cortex.

Theta waves: electrical activity of the brain typically associated with certain stages of sleep and with very deep states of relaxation, characterized by frequencies of four to eight hertz, or cycles per second.

Thyroid gland: a gland in the neck that secretes hormones involved in the regulation of metabolic rate.

Yoga: a school of Hindu philosophy. In the West, the term usually refers to a set of postures and exercises practiced to achieve total physical and mental fitness.

BIBLIOGRAPHY

BOOKS

Ambriere, Francis. *The Long Holiday*. Chicago: Ziff-Davis, 1948.

Above and Beyond (Library of Curious and Unusual Facts). Alexandria, Va.: Time-Life Books, 1992.

Abram, Stephen E., ed. *The Pain Clinic Manual*. Philadelphia: J. B. Lippincott Company, 1990.

Akil, Huda. "Endorphins/Enkephalins." In *Textbook of Internal Medicine* (2d ed.), ed. by W. N. Kelley. Philadelphia: J. B. Lippincott, 1991.

Anderson, Terry A. *Den of Lions: Memoirs of Seven Years*. New York: Crown, 1993.

Asterita, Mary F. *The Physiology of Stress*. New York: Human Sciences Press, 1985.

Baldry, P. E. *Acupuncture, Trigger Points and Musculoskeletal Pain*. New York: Churchill Livingstone, 1989.

Bannister, Roger. *The Four Minute Mile*. New York: Dodd, Mead, 1955.

Basbaum, Allan I. "The Generation and Control of Pain." In *Encyclopaedia Britannica, Medical Supplement*, ed. by E. Bernstein. Chicago: Encyclopaedia Britannica, 1987.

Benson, Herbert. *The Mind/Body Effect*. New York: Simon and Schuster, 1979.

Berkley, George E. *Hitler's Gift: The Story of Theresienstadt*. Boston: Branden Books, 1993.

Block, Gay, and Malka Drucker. *Rescuers: Portraits of Moral Courage in the Holocaust*. New York: Holmes and Meier, 1992.

Bloom, Floyd E., and Arlyne Lazerson. *Brain, Mind, and Behavior* (2d ed.). New York: W. H. Freeman, 1988.

Blueprint for Life (Journey Through the Mind and Body). Alexandria, Va.: Time-Life Books, 1993.

Boswell, John. *The U.S. Armed Forces Survival Manual*. New York: Times Books. 1980.

Bowers, Richard W., and Edward L. Fox. *Sports Psysiology* (3d ed.). Dubuque, Iowa: William C. Brown, 1992.

Brobeck, John R., Orr E. Reynolds, and Toby A. Appel (eds.). *History of the American Physiological Society*. Bethesda, Md.: American Physiological Society, 1987.

Burger, Jerry M. *Desire for Control: Personality, Social, and Clinical Perspectives*. New York: Plenum Press, 1992.

Butt, Dorcas Susan. *The Psychology of Sport*. New York: Van Nostrand Reinhold, 1987.

Campbell, Joseph. *The Historical Atlas of World Mythology, Vol. 1: The Way of the Animal Powers:*

Mythologies of the Primitive Hunters and Gatherers (Part 1). New York: Harper and Row, 1988.

Mythologies of the Great Hunt (Part 2). New York: Harper and Row, 1988.

Carroll, Marilyn. "PCP: The Dangerous Angel." *The Encyclopedia of Psychoactive Drugs*. New York: Chelsea House, 1985.

Chopra, Deepak. *Quantum Healing*. New York: Bantam Books, 1989.

Clayman, Charles B. (ed.). *American Medical Association Encyclopedia of Medicine*. New York: Random House, 1989.

Corey, Dr. David, with Stan Solomon. *Pain: Learning to Live without It*. Toronto: MacMillan Canada, 1993.

Cornum, Rhonda, and Peter Copeland. *She Went to War*. Novato, Calif.: Presidio Press, 1992.

Cotton, Dorothy H. G. *Stress Management: An Integrated Approach to Therapy*. New York: Brunner/Mazel, 1990.

Cousins, Norman. *Head First: The Biology of Hope*. New York: E. P. Dutton, 1989.

Craighead, Frank C., Jr., and John J. Craighead. *How to Survive on Land and Sea* (4th ed., rev.). Annapolis, Md.: Naval Institute Press, 1984.

Cruikshank, Jeffrey L. *A Delicate Experiment: The Harvard Business School, 1908-1945*. Boston: Harvard Business School Press, 1987.

Csikszentmihalyi, Mihaly. *Flow: The Psychology of Optimal Experience*. New York: Harper and Row, 1990.

Davis, Joel. *Endorphins: New Waves in Brain Chemistry*. New York: Doubleday, 1984.

Department of the Army. *Field Manual 21-76: Survival, Evasion and Escape*. Washington, D.C.: U.S. Government Printing Office, Mar. 14, 1969.

Diamond, A. W., and S. W. Coniam. *The Management of Chronic Pain*. New York: Oxford University Press, 1991.

Diamond, Marian C., Arnold B. Scheibel, and Lawrence M. Elson. *The Human Brain Coloring Book*. New York: HarperPerennial, 1985.

Di Pasquale, Mauro G. *Drug Use and Detection in Amateur Sports*. Warkworth, Ontario: M. G. D. Press, 1984.

Directory of Pain Treatment Centers in the U.S. and Canada. Phoenix: Oryx Press, 1989.

Dubal, David. *Reflections from the Keyboard*. New York: Summit Books, 1984.

Dunlevy, Maurice. *Stay Alive: A Handbook on Survival*. Canberra, Australia: Australian Government Publishing Service, 1978.

Elder, Lauren, with Shirley Streshinsky. *And I Alone Survived*. New York: E. P. Dutton, 1978.

Elton, Diana, Gordon Stanley, and Graham Burrows. *Psychological Control of Pain*. New York: Grune and Stratton, 1983.

Everly, George S., Jr., and Robert Rosenfeld. *The Nature and Treatment of the Stress Response*. New York: Plenum Press, 1981.

Fear, Gene. *Surviving the Unexpected Wilderness Emergency*. Takoma, Wash.: Survival Education Association, 1975.

Fields, Howard L. *Pain*. New York: McGraw-Hill, 1987.

Fisher, S. *Stress and the Perception of Control*. Hillsdale, N.J.: Lawrence Erlbaum Associates, 1984.

Fixx, James F. *Maximum Sports Performance*. New York: Random House, 1985.

Frankl, Viktor. *Man's Search for Meaning*. New York: Washington Square Press, 1963.

Gallwey, W. Timothy. *The Inner Game of Tennis*. New York: Random House, 1974.

Garfield, Charles A.:

Peak Performance. New York: Warner Books, 1984.

Peak Performers: The New Heroes of American Business. New York: William Morrow, 1986.

Gazzaniga, Michael S.:

Mind Matters: How Mind and Brain Interact to Create Our Conscious Lives. Boston: Houghton Mifflin, 1988.

Nature's Mind: The Biological Roots of Thinking, Emotions, Sexuality, Language, and Intelligence. New York: BasicBooks, 1992.

Goodbody, John. *The Illustrated History of Gymnastics*. London: Stanley Paul, 1982.

Hanson, Peter G. *Stress for Success*. New

York: Doubleday, 1989.

Hoberman, John M. *Mortal Engines: The Science of Performance and the Dehumanization of Sport.* New York: Free Press, 1992.

Holaday, John W. *Endogenous Opioids and Their Receptors.* Kalamazoo, Mich.: Upjohn, 1985.

Holden, A. V., and W. Winlow (eds.). *The Neurobiology of Pain.* Manchester, England: Manchester University Press, 1984.

The Incredible Machine. Washington, D.C.: National Geographic Society, 1986.

Japan (Library of Nations). Alexandria, Va.: Time-Life Books, 1985.

Kandel, Eric R., James H. Schwartz, and Thomas M. Jessell (eds.). *Principles of Neural Science* (3d ed.). New York: Elsevier, 1991.

Kapit, Wynn, Robert I. Macey, and Esmail Meisami. *The Physiology Coloring Book.* New York: HarperCollins, 1987.

Klausner, Samuel Z. (ed.). *Why Man Takes Chances.* New York: Anchor Books, 1968.

Kugelmann, Robert. *Stress: The Nature and History of Engineered Grief.* Westport, Conn.: Praeger, 1992.

Lazarus, Richard S., and Susan Folkman. *Stress, Appraisal, and Coping.* New York: Springer, 1984.

Maslow, Abraham H. *Toward a Psychology of Being* (2d ed.). New York: Van Nostrand Reinhold, 1982.

Medvei, Victor Cornelius. *A History of Endocrinology.* Hingham, Mass.: MTP Press, 1982.

Melzack, Ronald, and Patrick D. Wall. *The Challenge of Pain.* New York: Basic Books, 1982.

Mind and Brain (Journey Through the Mind and Body). Alexandria, Va.: Time-Life Books, 1993.

Moyers, Bill. *Healing and the Mind.* New York: Doubleday, 1993.

Muston, John. *Survival Training and Techniques.* New York: Arms and Armour Press, 1987.

Nabokov, Peter. *Indian Running: Native American History and Tradition.* Santa Fe, N.M.: Ancient City Press, 1981.

Oliner, Samuel P., and Pearl M. Oliner. *The Altruistic Personality.* New York: Free Press, 1988.

Orlick, Terry. *In Pursuit of Excellence* (2d ed.).

Champaign, Ill.: Leisure Press, 1990.

Parrino, John J. *From Panic to Power: The Positive Use of Stress.* New York: John Wiley and Sons, 1979.

Peale, Norman Vincent. *You Can If You Think You Can.* Englewood Cliffs, N.J.: Prentice-Hall, 1974.

Pease, Victor. *Anxiety into Energy.* New York: Elsevier-Dutton, 1981.

Petersen, Robert C., and Richard C. Stillman. *Phencyclidine (PCP) Abuse: An Appraisal.* Rockville, Md.: National Institute on Drug Abuse, 1978.

Restak, Richard M. *The Brain.* New York: Bantam Books, 1984.

Ridge, Julie, and Judith Zimmer. *Take It to the Limit.* New York: Rawson Associates, 1984.

Salmon, Paul G., and Robert G. Meyer. *Notes from the Green Room.* New York: Lexington Books, 1992.

Samuels, Mike, and Nancy Samuels. *Seeing with the Mind's Eye.* New York: Random House, 1975.

Sandweiss, Jack H., and Steven L. Wolf. *Biofeedback and Sports Science.* New York: Plenum Press, 1985.

Sastry, Padma. *Sherpas: The Brave Mountaineers.* Darjeeling, Nepal: Himalayan Mountaineering Institute, 1991.

Schultheis, Rob. *Bone Games: One Man's Search for the Ultimate Athletic High.* New York: Fromm, 1984.

Schwertfeger, Ruth (ed.). *Women of Theresienstadt: Voices from a Concentration Camp.* New York: Berg, 1989.

Scott, Doug. *Himalayan Climber: A Lifetime's Quest to the World's Greater Ranges.* San Francisco: Sierra Club Books, 1992.

Selye, Hans:
The Stress of Life (rev. ed.). New York: McGraw-Hill, 1976.
Stress without Distress. New York: J. B. Lippincott, 1974.

Shaffer, Martin. *Life After Stress.* New York: Plenum Press, 1982.

Shanks, Bernard. *Wilderness Survival* (rev. ed.). New York: Universe Books, 1987.

Simpson, Joe. *Touching the Void.* New York: Harper and Row, 1988.

Smith, David, et al. (eds.). *PCP: Problems and*

Prevention. Dubuque, Iowa: Kendall/Hunt Publishing, 1982.

The Sports Illustrated 1994 Sports Almanac. Boston: Little, Brown, 1994.

Stockdale, James B. *A Vietnam Experience.* Palo Alto, Calif.: Hoover Press Publications/Stanford University, 1984.

Tortora, Gerard J., and Ronald L. Evans. *Principles of Human Physiology* (2d ed.). New York: Harper and Row, 1986.

Tortora, Gerard J., and Sandra Reynolds Grabowski. *Principles of Anatomy and Physiology* (7th ed.). New York: HarperCollins, 1993.

Vander, Arthur J., James H. Sherman, and Dorothy S. Luciano. *Human Physiology: The Mechanisms of Body Function* (5th ed.). New York: McGraw-Hill, 1990.

Veninga, Robert L., and James P. Spradley. *The Work/Stress Connection: How to Cope with Job Burnout.* Boston: Little, Brown, 1981.

Volavková, Hana (ed.). *I Never Saw Another Butterfly: Children's Drawings and Poems from Terezín Concentration Camp, 1942-1944.* New York: McGraw-Hill, 1976.

Whitaker, Charlotte Sibley, and Donald Ray Tanner. *"But I Played It Perfectly in the Practice Room!"* New York: University Press of America, 1987.

Wright, James E., and Virginia S. Cowart. *Anabolic Steroids: Altered States.* Carmel, Ind.: Benchmark Press, 1990.

PERIODICALS

Allman, William F. "The Mental Edge." *U.S. News and World Report,* Aug. 3, 1992.

Axthelm, Pete. "Using Chemistry to Get the Gold." *Newsweek,* July 25, 1988.

Barinaga, Marcia. "Playing 'Telephone' with the Body's Message of Pain." *Science,* Nov. 13, 1992.

Begley, Sharon. "The Second Wind." *Newsweek,* July 27, 1992.

Bloom, Marc. "What Is Limit for Chinese Women?" *New York Times,* Sept. 28, 1993.

Brandon, Jeffrey E., J. Mark Loftin, and Jack Curry Jr. "Role of Fitness in Mediating Stress." *Perceptual and Motor Skills,* 1991, Vol. 73, pp. 1171-1180.

Carpenter, Betsy. "A Game of Cat and Mouse." *U.S. News and World Report,*

Oct. 10, 1988.

Cherry, Laurence. "On the Real Benefits of Eustress." *Psychology Today*, Mar. 1978.

Church, George J. "Flood, Sweat and Tears." *Time*, July 26, 1993.

Csikszentmihalyi, Mihaly. "A Response to the Kimiecik & Stein and Jackson Papers." *Journal of Applied Sport Psychology*, Sept. 1992.

Darley, John M., and C. Daniel Batson. "From Jerusalem to Jericho: A Study of Situational and Dispositional Variables in Helping Behavior." *Journal of Personality and Social Psychology*, 1973, Vol. 27, pp. 100-108.

Doig, Desmond. "Sherpaland, My Shangri-La." *National Geographic*, Oct. 1966.

Dubner, R., and M. A. Ruda. "Activity-Dependent Neuronal Plasticity Following Tissue Injury and Inflammation." *Trends in Neurosciences*, 1992, Vol. 15, no.3.

Dunning, Jennifer. "When a Pianist's Fingers Fail to Obey." *New York Times Biographical Service*, June 1981.

Engel, George. "Emotional Stress and Sudden Death." *Psychology Today*, Nov. 1977.

"Fast Comeback for a Quarterback with a Bad Back." *Discover*, Jan. 1987.

Fogelman, Eva, and Valerie Lewis Wiener. "The Few, the Brave, the Noble." *Psychology Today*, Aug. 1985.

Gallwey, W. Timothy, and Robert Kriegel. "Fear of Skiing." *Psychology Today*, Nov. 1977.

Gelman, David. "To the Emotional Rescue." *Newsweek*, Aug. 16, 1993.

Gliatto, Tom. "The Road Back." *People*, Dec. 7, 1992.

Greist, John H., et al. "Antidepressant Running." *Psychiatric Annals*, Mar. 1979.

Greist, John H., et al. "Running as Treatment for Depression." *Comprehensive Psychiatry*, Jan./Feb. 1979.

Hall, Craig R., Wendy M. Rodgers, and Kathryn A. Barr. "The Use of Imagery by Athletes in Selected Sports." *The Sports Psychologist*, 1990, Vol. 4, pp. 1-10.

Harvard Business School Alumni Bulletin. Summer 1946.

Hopson, Janet L. "A Pleasurable Chemistry." *Psychology Today*, July/Aug. 1988.

Houghton, Brenda. "The Will to Defeat Pain without End." *The Independent on Sunday*, Oct. 24, 1993.

"Humor In Psychotherapy: An Interview with Dr. William F. Fry." *Humor & Health Letter*, Nov./Dec. 1992.

Impoco, Jim. "The Subway May Be Safe, but Rush Hour Is Murder." *U.S. News and World Report*, July 23, 1990.

Jackson, Susan A. "Athletes in Flow: A Qualitative Investigation of Flow States in Elite Figure Skaters." *Journal of Applied Sport Psychology*, Sept. 1992.

Jackson, Susan A., and Glyn C. Roberts. "Positive Performance States of Athletes." *The Sport Psychologist*, June 1992.

Jeffrey, Scott. "When the *Pride of Baltimore* Sank, Eight Sailors Got a Crash Course in Ocean Survival." *People*, July 14, 1986.

Kiester, Edwin, Jr. "The Playing Fields of the Mind." *Psychology Today*, July 1984.

Kimiecik, Jay C., and Gary L. Stein. "Examining Flow Experiences in Sport Contexts." *Journal of Applied Sport Psychology*, Sept. 1992.

Kohn, Alfie:

"Beyond Selfishness." *Psychology Today*, Oct. 1988.

"Do Religious People Help More? Not So You'd Notice." *Psychology Today*, Dec. 1989.

"Evidence for a Moral Tradition." *Psychology Today*, Jan./Feb. 1989.

Krucoff, Carol. "Peak Performances: Elite Athletes Compete in Barcelona Despite Their Physical Impairments." *Washington Post*, Sept. 29, 1992.

Kuznik, Frank. "A Nightmare Drug." *Washingtonian*, Jan. 1985.

Lambert, Pam. "Trial By Deluge." *People*, July 26, 1993.

Lambert, Pam, and Don Nugent. "Cut or Die." *People*, Aug. 9, 1993.

Lawrence, Jay. "Broncos Try Run-and-Parachute in Order to Increase Team Speed." *Rocky Mountain News*, May 14, 1991.

Lederman, Richard J. "Performing Arts Medicine." *New England Journal of Medicine*, Jan. 26, 1989.

Leviton, Richard. "Healing Vibrations." *Yoga Journal*, Jan./Feb. 1994.

Lockwood, Alan H. "Medical Problems of Musicians." *New England Journal of Medicine*, Jan. 26, 1989.

Mansour, Alfred, et al. "Anatomy of CNS Opioid Receptors." *Trends in Neurosciences*, 1988, Vol. 11, pp. 308-314.

Melzack, Ronald, and Patrick D. Wall. "Pain Mechanisms: A New Theory." *Science*, Nov. 1965.

Meyer, Charles. "Forty-Five Minutes of Mozart, B.I.D.?" *American Journal of Nursing*, Feb. 1992.

"Moments." *Life*, Mar. 1992.

Nelson, Margaret, and Karen S. Schneider. "Comeback Kid." *People*, May 25, 1992.

Roberts, Marjory:

"Be All that You Can Be." *Psychology Today*, Mar. 1988.

"Eight Ways to Rethink." *Psychology Today*, Mar. 1989.

Rosellini, Lynn, John Marks, and Victoria Pope. "The Sports Factories." *U.S. News and World Report*, Feb. 17, 1992.

Rowes, Barbara. "Right Now Gary Graffman Will Settle for Being the World's Ranking One-Handed Piano Maestro." *People*, Apr. 6, 1981.

"Run and Chute." *Sports Illustrated*, May 27, 1991.

"A Savage Stalks at Midnight." *Time*, June 26, 1964.

Schrof, Joannie M. "Pumped Up." *U.S. News and World Report*, June 1, 1992.

Severance, Peter. "The Legend of the Tarahumara." *Runner's World*, Dec. 1993.

Shepherd, Paul. "The Torch of Technology: The Science Behind the '92 Olympics." *Omni*, July 1992.

Shotland, R. Lance. "When Bystanders Just Stand By." *Psychology Today*, June 1985.

Sinyor, David, et al. "Failure to Alter Sympathoadrenal Response to Psychosocial Stress Following Aerobic Training." *Physiology and Behavior*, 1988, Vol. 42, pp. 293-296.

Smith, Brad. "Legendary Runners." *Denver Post*, Aug. 26, 1993.

Snyder, Solomon H. "Drug and Neurotransmitter Receptors in the Brain." *Science*, Apr. 6, 1984.

Stark, Elizabeth. "Breaking the Pain Habit." *Psychology Today*, May 1985.

Suinn, Richard M. "Body Thinking: Psychology for Olympic Champs." *Psychology Today*, July 1976.

Torrey, Lee. "How Science Creates Winners." *Science*, Aug. 1984.

Toufexis, Anastasia. "Engineering the Perfect Athlete." *Time*, Aug. 3, 1992.

"Vereen, Back on Broadway." *Washington Post*, Apr. 10, 1993.

Vizard, Frank. "The Technology of the Olympics." *Popular Mechanics*, Feb. 1992.

Walker, Lou Ann. "A Place for Healing." *People*, Sept. 13, 1993.

Wang, Julie. "Breaking Out of the Pain Trap." *Psychology Today*, July 1977.

Warga, Claire. "Pain's Gatekeeper." *Psychology Today*, Aug. 1987.

Warner, Linda, and M. Evelyn McNeill. "Mental Imagery and Its Potential for Physical Therapy." *Physical Therapy*, Apr. 1988.

"War Work and Peace Plans of the Fatigue Laboratory." *Harvard Business School Alumni Bulletin*, Winter 1945.

Zimmerman, Paul. "The Ultimate Winner." *Sports Illustrated*, Aug. 13, 1990.

OTHER SOURCES

"Can Science Build a Champion Athlete?" NOVA television series, program #2006. Boston: WGBH Educational Foundation, Feb. 16, 1993.

Fry, William F., Jr.:
"Homeodynamics: A Lesson of Laughter." Abstract of a presentation at the 10th International Conference on Humor, Paris, France, July 1992.
"The Power of Humor." Abstract of address presented at Hospitalhof Stuttgart Evangelisches Bildungswerk, Stuttgart, Germany, Sept. 16, 1993.

"The Glory of the Games." Pamphlet for 1996 Paralympic Games. Atlanta: Atlanta Paralympic Organizing Committee, 1992.

"Key Word 'Survival'." Lesson outline. Fort Bragg, N.C.: U.S. Army John F. Kennedy Special Warfare Center and School, Feb. 1990.

"Physically Able." Old Spice Athlete of the Month advertisement in *Sports Illustrated*, May 3, 1993.

"Physiological and Psychological Aspects of Captivity." Lesson outline. Fort Bragg, N.C.: U.S. Army John F. Kennedy Special Warfare Center and School, Apr. 1992.

"Sports Mental Training: Relaxation and Energy Management for Athletes." Pamphlet prepared by Sports Psychology Department for U.S. Athletes. Colorado Springs: U.S. Olympic Committee, 1990.

Torrance, E. Paul. *Psychological Aspects of Survival*. Memorandum for the Human Factors Operations Research Laboratories (HFORL Memorandum #TN 54-4.). Ref. No. AD049626. Alexandria, Va.: Defense Technical Information Center, Jan. 1954.

United States Shooting Team 1993 Media Guide. Colorado Springs: U.S. Shooting Team, 1993.

INDEX

ACKNOWLEDGMENTS

The editors of *Tapping Hidden Power* wish to thank the following for their contributions:

Theresa Amiel, U.S. Holocaust Memorial Museum, Washington, D.C.; Allan I. Basbaum, University of California, San Francisco; Michael Berenbaum, U.S. Holocaust Memorial Museum; Lee Berk, Loma Linda University Medical Center, Loma Linda, Calif.; Peter Brancazio, Brooklyn College, Brooklyn; Jefferey Broker, U.S. Olympic Committee, Colorado Springs; Adrian Burden, West London Institute of Higher Education, London; Phil Cabral, British Association of Sports Sciences, Leeds, England; Lisa Cape, Atlanta Paralympic Organizing Committee, Atlanta; Paul E. Cook, Special Operations, Fort Bragg, N.C.; David Corey, Health Recovery Clinic, Toronto; Sonia Cozzi, Istituto Scienza dello Sport, Rome; Michael Crowley, Beltsville, Md.; Antonio Dal Monte, Istituto Scienza dello Sport, Rome; Darren Dutto, International Center for Aquatic Research, Colorado Springs;

Gary Elder, Washington, D.C.; Josep Escoda, Centre d'Alt Rendiment, San Cugat del Valles, Barcelona, Spain; Steven J. Fleck, U.S. Olympic Committee, Colorado Springs; Bob Foth, U.S. Olympic Shooting Center, Colorado Springs; William F. Fry Jr., Nevada City, Calif.; Daniel Gould, University of North Carolina at Greensboro; Paul Grimshaw, West London Institute of Higher Education, London; Laura Hitchcock, National Chronic Pain Outreach Association, Bethesda, Md.; Gary Hutzell, Vienna, Va.; Istituto di Scienza dello Sport, Rome; Carol Jones, Special Operations, Fort Bragg, N.C.; Ken Kline, Biovision, Menlo Park, Calif.; Daniel M. Landers, Arizona State University, Tempe, Ariz.; John D. Loeser, University of Washington Medical Center, Seattle; Sabine Maas, Deutsche Sporthochschule, Cologne, Germany; Sean C. McCann, U.S. Olympic Committee, Colorado Springs; Kenneth McGraw, Special Operations, Fort Bragg, N.C.; Genya Markon, U.S. Holocaust Memorial Museum; Kathleen Sharon Matt,

Arizona State University, Tempe; Astrid Michler, Michler Bild-Archiv, Balzheim, Germany; Annette Miller, Health Recovery Clinic, Toronto; John Moffett, Georgetown University, Washington, D.C.; Don W. Morgan, University of North Carolina at Greensboro; Calvin Morriss, Manchester Metropolitan University, Cheshire, England; Peter Ostwald, University of California, San Francisco; Steven Philbrick, Seattle; Antonio Prat, Centre d'Alt Rendiment, San Cugat del Valles, Barcelona, Spain; Gary Ruper, Sensory Environment Engineers, Fontana, Calif.; Sarah L. Smith, U.S. Olympic Committee, Colorado Springs; Carlos Suarez-Quian, Georgetown University Medical Center, Washington, D.C.; Paolo Valpolini, Milan, Italy; Tony Wolpentest, Mountain Lake Terrace, Wash.; Elizabeth Warren, Fairchild Air Force Base, Spokane; Kevin Working, Special Operations, Fort Bragg, N.C.; Diane L. Wyland, Frederick, Md.; Fred Yeadon, Loughborough University, Leicestershire, England.

PICTURE CREDITS

Cover: David Madison/Duomo Photography, Inc. **7:** Ron Haviv/SABA—Comstock, Inc./Gary Benson—Ronald C. Modra/ Sports Illustrated. **8, 9:** ©Arizona Daily Star. **11:** Photo by Bill Will, courtesy Gregory P. Robertson—AP/Wide World. **12:** Wide World Photos. **14:** UPI/Bettman—People Weekly, ©1974 John Olson. **16:** Michael Siegel/Phototake. **17:** ©1978 Los Angeles Times. **20:** ©Harald Sund. **21:** Lois Ellen Frank/Westlight. **22:** ©Don Spiro/Tony Stone Images. **23:** Anthony Suau/Gamma-Liaison International. **25:** ©Bruce Paul Richards. **26:** The Bettmann Archive. **28, 29:** Ron Haviv/SABA. **31:** ©Tim Davis. **33:** From *Rescuers: Portraits of Moral Courage in the Holocaust*, Gay Block and Malka Drucker, Holmes & Meier, New York, 1992. **35-43:** Art by Stephen R. Wagner. **44, 45:** Photo Affairs Jürgen Bögelsphaher, Bad Dürrheim, Foto: B. Haller. **46, 47:** People Weekly, ©1992 Taro Yamasaki. **49-51:** Art by Stephen R. Wagner. **52:** Courtesy Professor

Patrick D. Wall, London—courtesy Ronald Melzack. **56, 57:** Dr. William E. Siri, ©National Geographic Society; Doug Scott, Low Cotehill, Cumbria. **58, 59:** Art by Alfred T. Kamajian; Dennis Kunkel/Phototake. **61:** Mary Ellen Mark/Library. **63:** Geoffrey Gove/Image Bank. **65:** Charley Franklin/FPG International. **67:** ©Comstock, Inc./Michael Stuckey, 1994. **68, 69:** Charley Franklin/FPG International. **70:** Centre de Documentation Juive Contemporaine, Paris, courtesy the United States Holocaust Memorial Museum. **71:** Courtesy the State Jewish Museum, Prague, photographed by Antonín Novy. **72:** Dominique Aubert/Sygma. **74, 75:** George F. Mobley, ©National Geographic Society. **76, 77:** Kip Brundage/Woodfin Camp, Inc. **78, 79:** Comstock, Inc. **80, 81:** Kaz Chiba/Photonica. **82, 83:** Comstock, Inc./Gary Benson. **84, 85:** Steve Edson/Photonica. **86, 87:** ©1993 Felix Rigau, San Francisco, image manipulation by Time-Life Books. **88, 89:** Ronald C. Modra/Sports Illustrated. **91:** Casey Gibson. **92, 93:** Press Association, London; David Madison/Duomo Photography, Inc. **95:** Baker Library, Harvard University

Graduate School of Business Administration. **97:** GES Pressefoto, Karlsruhe. **98-100:** Art by Alfred T. Kamajian. **103:** U.S. Olympic Committee-Sport Science. **105:** David Madison/Duomo Photography, Inc. **106:** Dennis O'Clair/Tony Stone Images. **109:** Carl Yarbrough. **110, 111:** Stefan Warter/ Sports. **113:** ©Richard Fisher. **114, 115:** Handicap Bildagentur/Emanuel Bloedt, Dortmund—Chris Hamilton; ©Rich Frishman. **116, 117:** G. Rancinan/Sygma. **118:** People Weekly, ©1981 Henry Grossman. **120, 121:** Walter Schmitz/Bilderberg. **122, 123:** Background Carl Yarbrough; ©Dave Black (2). **124, 125:** Oswald Eckstein/Okapia, Frankfurt—Daniel M. Landers (2); Duomo Photography, Inc. (2). **126, 127:** Allsport—David Madison/Duomo Photography, Inc. **128, 129:** ©Dave Black; United States Swimming International Center for Aquatic Research (4). **130:** Dave Black/ Sports Photo Masters, Inc.—USOC, Sport Science & Technology Division, using Peak Performance Technologies' Motion Measurement Software. **131:** ©Dave Black— Peak Performance Technologies, Inc., Englewood, Colo. (2). **132, 133:** Biovision.